WHISTLING CI

WHISTLING CLOUGH

by

WALTER UNSWORTH

CICERONE PRESS
MILNTHORPE, CUMBRIA

© Walt Unsworth 1970
First published by Victor Gollancz Ltd 1970
This edition published by Cicerone Press 1989

ISBN 1 85284 046 3 (Hardback)
ISBN 1 85284 044 7 (Paperback)

Text printed and bound by Butler & Tanner Ltd.,
Frome, Somerset, England

All this country is hollow. Could you strike it with some gigantic hammer it would boom like a drum.

Sir Arthur Conan Doyle

CONTENTS

CHAPTER ONE

Brett Assheton

A wisp of blue grey smoke curled lazily in the
evening air, hung suspended for a moment, and
then vanished on the lightest of breezes. It came
from a hollow in a fold of the limestone moors, away
from the curious eyes of any stranger who happened
to be passing that way. It was almost invisible
against the fading light.

The boy had smelt the smoke as he jogged his
tired old nag up the steep, rutted path—just the
faintest whiff, caught for a second on a passing air,
then gone, but it was sufficient to make him draw
rein and look for its source. He was tired, for he had
ridden a long way that day, and his horse, well past
its prime of life, was tired, too. Uncertain as to his
exact whereabouts, he looked at the greying, inhospitable curves of Middleton Moor with some
distaste.

"What a God-forsaken place this Derby is, to be
sure," he thought, and not for the first time that day.
Unless he found his uncle's house within the hour
he could foresee himself spending a chill October
night in the open. That was a thought he would
rather not dwell upon, for although he was a tall

1*

and well-built youth for his sixteen years, and one of
Nature's more reckless creations, he had heard that
there were things on the moor at night which would
daunt the bravest souls.

He eyed the curling smoke reflectively. Whoever
had lit the fire had not wished to be seen—a gypsy
perhaps? Or a foot-pad? The boy loosened his dust-
stained cloak and felt beneath it for the reassurance
of the pistol which his father had given him for the
journey. It was an old weapon, one which his father
had bought for self-protection twenty years
previously when the Young Pretender and his
wild Highlanders had marched down from Scot-
land in a bid for the Crown, but it worked well
enough. Enough to blow a gaping hole through a
villain at twenty paces, with luck and a good aim.

The boy gave a determined shrug, and hitched
his saddlebags more into position as if the act
reflected his determination. He would face the
mysterious fire-lighter—after all, it was probably
some farm labourer burning rubbish who would be
able to direct him to his uncle's house.

He ambled the old nag forward and where the
track wound round to enter into a narrow valley
cutting deep into the moor, he pulled to one side,
toiling up the steep grass flanks of a small knoll
which separated him from the smoke. He rode
slowly, quietly, until at last he could peer down into
the hollow.

Below him was a shallow bowl of turf broken here
and there by white flecks of limestone where the
bare bones of the land poked through the thin

grassy skin. In the centre of this bowl a small twig fire was glowing and standing over the fire was a huge figure of a man, carefully carving the hind leg off a recently butchered sheep. He did it as one skilled in the craft, his knife making quick, incisive cuts into the dead animal, without waste or mistake, undeterred by blood. With a final thrust, the leg was severed and the rest of the carcase dropped, unwanted, to the ground. The giant, for giant he seemed, examined the mutton he had so crudely obtained, gave a grunt of satisfaction and thrust it into the embers. Without bothering to clean his knife, he folded it away into a capacious jacket pocket.

The boy watched, fascinated and apprehensive. One thing was sure—the fellow was no beauty: a great shambling ape whose lank black hair hung greasily down to the nape of his neck where it rested on a filthy red kerchief. His face was an unwashed brown and looked as though it had been trodden on by the world in general, and the fact that he had not shaved for several days lent it a sinister veneer. His massive body seemed as if it might burst at any moment from the confines of his old blue jacket, and his breeches, stained beyond colouring, scarcely met the tops of his hooped and darned hose. On his feet he wore clogs of the common sort.

That the man was a vagabond and a rogue was readily apparent, and yet the quick eye of the boy detected that for all that the man's face had not the hard set of a real villain. Some humanity lingered, like a small plant flowering in a vast desert.

The boy dismounted and slid so quietly down the grassy bank that the other had no knowledge of his presence.

"Good evening to you, sir," said the boy.

The big man jumped back, dropped the leg of mutton, and let out a violent oath. For a moment it seemed that he would spring on his intruder, full of savage fight, but then it dawned on him that it was a mere boy who had spoken and his huge frame relaxed, though his eyes remained watchful.

"Damme, young 'un, but tha startled me," he growled in a rough dialect.

"I'm sorry," replied the boy civilly, "but I'm come out of my way and seeing your fire, thought to seek directions for my journey."

The big man eyed him thoughtfully for a moment, then turned back to the cooking of his supper. "Tha looks clemmed," he said. "Hast etten today?"

"Not much," replied the boy, squatting down on the turf near the giant.

"Theer's enough here for both on us, ah reckons." He broke a piece of sizzling crisp mutton from the leg with one twist of his enormous dirty paw and handed it to the boy, who took it and hungrily attacked the succulent meat. The man himself knawed at the rest of the leg, eyeing the boy speculatively while he did so. The lad was big, almost six feet, he noted, with a handsome face and black curly hair down to the nape of his neck. His clothes were good, of the yeoman sort, though much stained with travelling, and he wore heavy shoes buckled in brass. He was obviously not afraid of his surroundings, despite the fact that they were remote and forbidding on this autumn evening. There seemed to be a stubbornness about his mouth and an awareness in his dark grey eyes, which struck a spark of appreciation in the big man.

"Yon's a stolen sheep tha eating," he said in his gruff voice. "Ah sees no sense i' payin' for meight when theer's plenty walkin' round on foor legs."

The boy continued to chew the mutton. With a mouth half full he said, "Stealing sheep is a hanging matter."

"Aye, and so is eatin' it."

The boy laughed at this and the ugly face of his companion responded with a half grin which revealed broken and tobacco-stained teeth.

"What's tha name, young 'un?" the giant demanded.

"Brett Assheton," replied the boy. "What's yours?"

"Folk caws me Black Jake o' Langsett—a sougher by way of profession."

"That's a trade I've never heard tell of afore," said the boy.

"Sougher? Why, he's a chap as drives soughs— tunnels for drainin' t'flood watter from t'lead mines. Hast ne'er heerd tell on Calver Sough or Mags-clough Sough?"

" 'Fraid not, sir. The ways of lead mining are foreign to me."

" 'Tis best left that way, then. Theer's better roads on earnin' a livin' than diggin' for lead, tak my word for it. Stay above ground, young 'un, and leave the burrowing to rats and moles, as God intended!"

Brett smiled but said nothing and the big man continued. "Ony road, theer's nowt in it for t'likes o' me and thee, these days. Time was when a chap wi a hack an' a wedge could dig hissel' a fortune, but not no moor. See yon chimbleys?" He pointed to the distance where Brett could discern faint smudges of smoke. "Yon's Eyam, wheer theer's as rich a vein as mon could wish for: Highcliffe Mine, Middleton Engine, New Engine, Morewood Engine—aw big enterprises, lad, wi' rich folk like the Bradshaws and Wrights ownin' 'em. Aye, and city companies like the Northern Mining Company, built, they tells me, wi' bits o' papper cawed share certificates or some such nonsense."

"But there must be smaller enterprises—run by families I mean?"

Black Jake snorted in contempt. "A few—them as hasn't sowd out. Most on 'em do a bit o' farmin' on t'side to mak a livin'. Tak this place—belongs to Owd Will Booth of Whistling Clough; spends hafe his time wi' sheep and t'rest in yon owd mine he's getten."

Seeing a sudden change come over the boy's countenance, Black Jake stopped his discourse. "What ails thee?" he asked.

Brett's face had hardened in such a way as to make the other man wary.

"Will Booth is my uncle," said Brett. " 'Twas Whistling Clough I was seeking when I saw your fire."

"Why, then—tha's found thi way," said Black Jake slowly. He lumbered to his feet but Brett sprang up and away from him, as agile as a cat.

" 'Tis not so simple, sir," he said. "There's a matter of a stolen sheep."

The big man nodded. "There's a matter o' a stolen and *eaten* sheep," he corrected, meaningly.

They stood facing each other at five paces, each searching the other's countenance for some sign of submission and finding none. In the short time of their acquaintance Brett had acquired a sneaking regard for this huge hulk of a man, villain though he undoubtedly was, and Black Jake, for his own part, felt a strange admiration for this foreigner who wandered alone in Peakland. Not that either would have admitted as much. They stared at each other with hostility.

It was Brett who made a gesture of friendship. "Perhaps the sheep was not one of Uncle Will's, but a stray," he said. His voice carried no conviction and he did not believe it himself for one moment.

Black Jake brushed the gesture aside. He had no time for excuses, no sympathy for cowards.

"It were Will Booth's sheep," he said deliberately. "It bore his mark."

Brett could have had him hung for that sentence. He wondered whether the boy would blab, but he thought not; if he judged his man rightly, Brett Assheton would settle this his own way. He wondered what the boy would do. Stand and fight? The odds were uneven, but he looked a likely lad— and well built.

"Then if 'twas my uncle's sheep I am bound by my family honour to protect his property, sir. You must pay for it."

A look of utter astonishment came over Black Jake's face.

"Pay for it?" he repeated in disbelief at what he'd heard.

"Aye—a guinea will suffice, I reckon."

Black Jake's ugly face widened into a grin, then he threw back his shaggy head and roared with laughter.

"A guinea! A guinea, no less!" He held his sides and tears of mirth ran down his dirty cheeks. "By all the saints but that's a rich one!" It was a minute or two before he could compose himself, then, wiping his eyes and still grinning he said, "And what if I don't choose to pay, me young bucko?"

"You'll pay," said the boy with a hard smile. "Because I have a pistol." And he drew the long pistol from beneath his cloak, pointing it directly at the big man's chest.

Black Jake's grin died a swift death. He looked at the pointing pistol, then at Brett's countenance. There was no doubt that Brett meant to have his guinea. Jake fumbled in a pocket and drew out a golden coin.

"Tha mun tak hafe a guinea—'tis aw ah've getten," he growled and tossed the coin across. Brett caught it deftly with his free hand.

" 'Twill suffice, no doubt," he said.

"Suffice? Hafe a golden guinea for a scraggy

sheep? By God! Yon's the dearest mutton i'
England!"

"Ah, but it pays for the salvation of your soul as
well, does it not, sir? It seems to me cheap at the
price."

Brett backed away until he reached his patiently
waiting nag. He slipped the pistol into his breeches
again, mounted his horse and gave a cheery wave of
his tricorne hat.

"Many thanks for your hospitality, good sir," he
cried. "Perhaps we may meet again—till then,
adieu!" He spurred his horse and quickly disappeared round a bend in the path.

For several minutes Black Jake just stood,
numbed by his experience. Then he cursed, softly
but vehemently. He cursed sheep, foreigners,
ingrates, Whistling Clough, Will Booth and Brett
Assheton. He even cursed Brett's mother for
bearing such a child. This seemed to relieve his
feelings and at the end of it he grinned philosophic-
ally. "Yon's a hard lad," he muttered to himself.
"And theer's some folk i' these parts as'll hev to
watch theer step from now on!"

Brett Assheton rode up to Whistling Clough, his
uncle's house, as the last rays of evening light were
glinting off the stone-shingled roof. The farmhouse
was bigger than the boy had imagined it would be,
long and low with deeply set windows as though it
was huddling against the inhospitable moor. It was
built on a limestone shelf in the bottom of the little
valley or clough from which it took its name, and on

two sides the steep slopes of the valley protected it from the elements. To its rear it was guarded by a clump of wind-stunted trees, but the front of the house, facing down the valley, was completely open, like a fortress commanding an approach to the moor. Already, lamps were lit in the downstairs rooms and the mullioned windows gleamed as yellow eyes. To the travel-weary Brett, the scene was one of welcome.

Uncle Will Booth was a broad, florid man with a bald head and squashed pug nose. When he smiled he meant it and Brett took a liking to him at once.

"He's coom," Uncle Will announced without formality and in a deep Derbyshire voice. "Our Mary's lad, young Brett. Coom along in, lad." And he led the way into a comfortably furnished room, lit by oil lamps and the glow from a large inglenook fire.

"Meet thi cousin Abigail."

Brett was stunned by the girl's beauty. She was fifteen or sixteen at a guess, small and neat and with a face which was perfectly shaped, with laughing brown eyes and rosebud mouth. Her hair, done into ringlets, was a lustrous brown tinged with just the hint of copper which took up and outmatched the russet silk of the dress she wore. Brett, dirty and unkempt from his long journey, felt awkward and abashed.

"Pleased to meet you, Cousin Brett," the girl said in a pleasant voice, touching his hand and making just the hint of a curtsey. "We feared you had lost your way and might not arrive till morning."

He remembered his drawing room manners just in time. He took her hand and kissed it, making a polite bow. "Your servant, Cousin," he replied. Abigail Booth blushed a little and smiled, and her father laughed good-naturedly.

"Why! Damme lad, but tha's made the wench colour. We're noan used to many visitors at Whistling Clough, and specially not educated young bucks, eh Abby?"

At this the girl blushed deeper and Will Booth teased her further. "Theer's no harm done lass," he said laughingly. "But Brett's a well set up young mon, and he comes wi' a reputation by aw accounts."

Now it was Brett's turn to colour. "I'm afraid that I arrive under a cloud, sir," he murmured, shamefacedly. "A disgrace to the family."

"Stuff and nonsense, lad!" cried a sharp voice from the inglenook. "Thi Uncle Will here were just as nowty when he were a young 'un."

Brett turned and saw for the first time that a grey-haired old lady, dressed in black silk, occupied the comfortable niche by the fire. Her face was like old parchment, with a fine nose and sharp eyes, and in her younger days she must have been something of a beauty.

"And this is Grandmother Booth," said Will, by way of introduction.

"Your servant, ma'am," said Brett.

"Stuff!" said the old lady, tartly. "Tha noan my

servant—tha mi grandchilt, and tha mun caw me granny same as aw God-fearin' childer should. I reckons nowt on aw these fancy city manners." Though she spoke sharply, she meant it kindly, as her eyes showed well enough. "And what does tha mean—a disgrace to t'family?"

Brett shifted his feet uncomfortably. He thought his father had explained the situation in a letter to his uncle, but here he was having to tell the sorry tale over again.

"I was sent down from the Academy at Warrington, ma'am—Granny, I mean."

"Tscha!" snorted the old lady in derision. "Ah blames thi fayther for sending thee to such a canting Quaker schoo' in t'fust place. Warrington Academy indeed!"

"But you know that since we are Non-comformists, Granny, we cannot attend the colleges of Oxford and Cambridge. They are only for members of the Established Church—we must seek our education elsewhere—and the Quaker college at Warrington has a fine reputation."

"Tha con read and write plain English, and count thi brass?"

"Aye, granny."

"Then tha's getten education enough. I don't howd wi aw this heathen Latin and Greek—'tis fit only for furriners and Papists!"

Will Booth laughed outright at his mother's views on education. "Pay no heed to her, lad," he advised. "Tell us why tha was chucked out o' yon Academy."

"Twere on account of Dr Priestley, of whom you have possibly heard tell. He had an argument with the Governors of the Academy and they dismissed him. I took Priestley's part in an argument over the rights and wrongs of the affair and it ended in a stand-up fight with fellow students on Warrington Bridge."

"How mony did tha feight?" demanded the old woman from the corner.

"There were five of 'em, granny," said Brett.

"And did tha beat 'em?"

"I gave a good account of myself. There were some bloodied noses and one fellow ended in the river."

The old lady cackled with glee. "Good lad! Good lad! Theer's nowt ah likes better than a good feight!"

Will Booth remonstrated with his mother, though he could scarcely keep a smile from his face.

"Nah then, Granny, don't thee egg him on. Feightin' in t'streets is no road for scholars to carry on."

"Stuff!" retorted the indomitable Mrs Booth.

"And they sent you away, just for fighting?" exclaimed Abby, full of sympathy for her handsome cousin.

"Aye, but as you may know, cousin, Quakers don't hold with fighting under any circumstances."

"Pap bellied hypocrites!" commented the old lady from her corner.

"Nah then, less o' that," said Will Booth. "Tha't an owd rogue, Granny Booth. Tha knows full weel that tha's as full o' admiration for t'Quakers as ony on us. They've getten their principles and they abides by 'em."

Brett had been sent to Derbyshire in disgrace, and there was no point in holding back any of his misdemeanors.

"Then there was the poaching," he said, lamely.

"Poaching?" His Uncle looked up in surprise. "Thi fayther's letter said nowt about poachin'. Sent away from t'Academy, and feightin' wi' t'village beadle on one occasion—but nowt about poachin'."

" 'Twere after the letter was despatched, uncle. I was in a tavern one evening with these two fellows and they laid bets that I dare not try snaring a rabbit on Lord Sefton's estate."

Granny Booth let out a whoop of high glee. "How mony didst tha ketch, lad?" She demanded.

"Three, Granny—as fine buck rabbits as ever you are likely to see."

The old lady clapped her hands in delight.

"Unfortunately, the local Constable caught me. My father paid him five guineas to forget the affair but it made my banishment to Derbyshire more certain than ever. Doubtless my father has informed you, sir, that I am to be put to some useful work. He believes that the harshness of the country hereabouts will help to tame my high spirits."

Will Booth nodded. "Wild nature against wild nature. Aye, well happen he's reet. Tha'll find it wild enough up on Middleton Moor, and no mistake. As for work, well 'tis true that owd Seth and me could do wi another pair o' honds at Whistling Clough Mine, but ah'm noan drivin' thee to it. Lead minin' is a hard life and tha mun coom to it gradual."

When Brett had washed and changed he joined the Booth family for supper, a homely but substantial meal of mutton chops and ham pie, washed down with tankards of home brewed ale. The meal was cooked and served by Mrs Hallam, a mournful soul who acted as housekeeper to the family and who gave as good as she got from old Granny Booth, who seemed to use her as a regular verbal sparring partner.

Now that he had time to find his bearings, Brett discovered that Whistling Clough was much more comfortable than Black Jake had led him to expect. Whatever the position of small lead miners-cum-farmers in general, the Booth family were obviously fairly well provided for. The house was flagged throughout, and though most of the furniture was of the solid farmhouse type, there were upholstered armchairs and even a bookcase with an assortment of leather-bound books. On one wall hung a remarkable, though unfinished, portrait of his Cousin Abigail, painted, she said, "by an itinerant artist: a handsome young fellow called George Romney."

During the meal the talk was of family affairs. Will's wife had died some years previously, and Abby was an only child—a fact which distressed old Granny Booth, because Will had refused to re-marry and there was no male heir to the land and mine. Will asked about his sister—Brett's mother—whom he had not seen in the twenty years since she had gone to Lancashire and married Brett's father. And in the way of such things the family talk drifted on and on in ever widening circles embracing aunts and uncles, distant cousins and long-forgotten nephews, until Brett, who entered the conversation whenever he could, felt wholly and completely one of the family.

After supper, Abby retired to bed and Brett, too, tired by his long day's ride went up to his room.

Will Booth sat looking into the log fire and wondering about the boy who had entered his home. Would Derbyshire and the life of a miner calm the youth? More important, would Brett like his new life, or would it crush him until he came to hate it? Will hoped not. He could see in Brett the son he never had.

"Yon's a high spirited lad," he said slowly, putting the worst of the case, as is North Country custom.

Granny Booth nodded. "A bit wild by aw accounts," she agreed, "but he's noan daft. He's getten brains and he's getten brawn—so what moor dust tha want i' a lad?"

"He's noan getten a feelin' for t'moors, and he's noan been browt up on lead. It maks a difference. Feightin' don't signify nowt. Its lead as counts i' these parts: lead, lead, lead!" And he thumped the arm of his chair passionately. "It allus has and allus will. Happen Derbyshire will break him."

There was a discreet knock on the door and Brett, in shirt sleeves, re-entered the room. To his uncle he proffered a half-guinea.

"It all but slipped my memory, sir," he said, by way of explanation, "but this is rightfully yours. I took it from a rogue whom I found stealing one of your sheep. He disliked paying but I persuaded him with my pistol."

And with a cheery good-night, he left the room, leaving his amazed uncle holding the golden coin.

Old Granny Booth was besides herself with delight. "What was tha saying, Will?" she mocked. "That Derby would break Brett Assheton? Why, at hafe a guinea a sheep, by my reckonin' Brett Assheton will break Derby!"

And she almost collapsed with laughter.

CHAPTER TWO

A Fight at The Moon

IN THE BRIGHT sparkling sunshine of morning the moor looked a different place altogether than it had on the previous evening. Brett and Abby, already friends, had walked up the Clough, until at last, tiring of the confines of the narrow little valley they had made a mad scramble, chasing one another like dog and hare, up the slopes to the moor itself.

It was much greener than Brett had imagined: the hills had the emerald tints of limestone-fed grass with an occasional long white wall dividing one property from another. Only the higher parts were brown, where the heather, already dying, took pride of place over the grass. Not that there were any hills in the real sense—more like long swellings of uplands which interlocked one with another in endless variety.

There were no trees, nor any houses that Brett could see, but here and there he could spy mounds of raw earth, maybe fifteen or twenty feet in height, like giant mole hills, with a few rude stone huts and primitive winches.

"Are those the lead mines?" Brett asked.

Abby nodded, her ringlets shaking prettily.

"They spoil the moor," she said sadly. "But for those horrible mines it would be beautiful up here. What is it that Mr Pope says in one of his poems? 'All around is beautiful and only man is vile.' That's true."

"I would not say so," Brett replied. "To a stranger like me they show the indomitable spirit of man. Here is this wild place, and yet here also is man wresting a living out of it: surely that is noble?"

"Tscha! Any savage is noble, or so they say! There's nothing noble about lead mining, sir; 'tis dirty, hard and cruel." She spoke so strongly that Brett protested.

"But for those very reasons 'tis noble, Abby. Think of the courage and endurance needed to wrest the raw metal from the binding rock! Think how man, a creature of daylight, fights in the darkness of the pit against mother earth herself. Why, there's a challenge!"

"Only a man would be stupid enough to think like that!"

Brett smiled. The fact that Abby had called him a man took away the insult.

"Look there," he said, changing the subject. "Somebody has cut a great dyke across the moor!" And it was true enough. A wide ditch, embanked on either hand, curled over the side of the hill for no apparent purpose.

"That's Dirty Rake," Abby said, and seeing her companion still puzzled she explained. "Sometimes a vein of lead ore comes out to the surface, and the

easiest way to mine it is simply to dig it out, following the vein across the moor. 'Tis called a rake, and
some are very old and famous, and the miners give
them names."

"A man who discovers a rake would be passing
rich!" exclaimed Brett enthusiastically. "Why fancy
—just digging up lead!"

Abby laughed and answered, "Aye—but 'tis only
a dream which rarely comes true. Rakes like that
yonder are not so readily found these days. Remember, sir, that men have been searching these moors
for lead since the days of Caesar. Aye! And probably
before that too. Today the lead lies deeper."

Brett's hopes of immediate wealth were dashed.
"Still, I wouldn't mind trying," he said wistfully.

"There's nought to stop you," Abby replied. "A
pick and a strong back is all that's required."

"And the land," added the boy with feeling.
"One would need to buy the land to work on."

" 'Tis easy to tell you are not a Peakrill," Abby
replied, "or you would not show such ignorance of
our laws and customs. Land you do *not* need. 'Tis
the law hereabouts that any man may dig for lead
whereso'er he wishes, and none may say nay to
him."

"But that's incredible!"

"But the truth nevertheless. Article Thirteen of
the Code says explicitly, 'It is lawful for all people
to dig Ore in any Ground whatever'—and believe
me, sir, in these parts we live by the Code!"

Brett, who had been brought up to regard the
Common Law of England as the be-all and end-all

of Justice throughout the Kingdom was thoroughly shocked. "Do you mean to tell me that you have your own *laws*?" he demanded.

Abby looked at him as though he was a simpleton. "But of course," she said with dignity. "We are not common folk—*we are lead miners*!"

That evening Uncle Will came home from a day's work at the mine and Brett had never seen a man so transformed. Gone was the honest yeoman's suit and the scrubbed, cheery face: to look at him Uncle Will resembled a footpad more than a prosperous farmer. His clothes were rough and dirty, his hands and face daubed with caked mud. He shook off his clogs on the stone-floored kitchen and came straight through to the drawing room where the rest of the family had gathered.

"Tha should wash thisel Will afore tha cooms i't'drawing room," said old Mrs Booth as he entered. By way of reply he drew from his pocket a piece of rock and handed it to her.

"It's takken Seth and me aw day to win a dish o'yon." He said.

She examined the rock and handed it back.

"It's noan good quality," she said.

"Ah knows that," he replied irritably. "There's moor muck than lead i'it, but what con a mon do agen Nature?"

"It's fra Top Level?"

"Aye, wheer else? Ah tells thee—every month yon Level is harder for t'work. Seth reckons yon vein is closing in on us."

With a gesture of distaste he shoved the rock into his pocket. "We mon try to open t'Bottom Level agen." He declared firmly.

Abby gave a little start. "The Bottom Level has been closed for years," she exclaimed. "It's deep and dangerous."

"Happen it is, dowter—but theer's nowt much left i' Top Level."

The girl seemed angry and perplexed. "A pox on the mine!" She cried. "I wish 'twere abandoned!"

"Abigail!" Her grandmother cried, properly shocked. "A young lady must ne'er swear. Shame on thee!"

"Who's the lady?" the girl cried bitterly. "Just because I have some education? I'm a miner's daughter, that's all I am!"

"Howd thi tongue wench!" her father cried angrily. "Happen th'art a miner's dowter, but ah'm a free miner for aw that, wi me own pit. What dost tha think pays for aw this?" and he swept his arm to indicate the comfortable room. "It were t'lead mine as built this house o'er a hun'red years since, an' has kept it goin'—aye and paid for thi schoolin'!"

"But there's the sheep—" his daughter protested.

"Aye, theer's t'sheep, and ah'm noan denyin' we've getten a good flock, but us Booths are miners and allus have been. Sheep is awreet—but 'tis lead as counts and doan't thee forget it!" And he went out of the room, banging the door behind him.

Abby sobbed and ran to her grandmother who put

her thin old arms round the girl and comforted her.

"Tha's still a lot for t'learn," said the old woman, stroking Abby's hair soothingly, "especially about menfolk. Don't let it upset thi, lass. But tha mon ne'er suggest abandonin' t'mine. Why tha met as weel suggest tha fayther cuts off his reet arm."

"I hate the mine!" Abby sobbed.

"Happen so, happen so, but 'tis best not to say as much to t'menfolk. Lead is a queer stuff lass. It's moor than just an owd bit o'metal—it's a way o'life."

"A way of death, more like!"

"Aye, theer's Booths hev deed seekin' lead."

"In the Bottom Level!"

" 'Tis true. But theer's nowt us women can do about it. T'Bottom Level has allus been a magnet for t'men o' t'Booth family. 'Tis said to be rich in t'finest ore. Happen it is, happen not. But they've got to *try*, dosn't see?"

The girl shook her head and turned from her grandmother to Brett, who had been a silent and embarrassed witness of the scene.

"You're not a miner, Brett. You're not a mole in a hole! Tell them 'tis folly to go to the Bottom Level. Tell father he's chasing fool's gold!"

But Brett shook his head. "A man must do as he thinks best," he said slowly.

"Men!" cried the girl, and stormed out of the room slamming the door for a second time.

Brett flushed and looked awkward. Old Mrs Booth cackled and cried, "Ne'er thee mind lad— her'll soon get o'er it."

Brett nodded. Then he said, "Tell me about the Bottom Level—"

And old Mrs Booth cackled again.

The following day Uncle Will sent Brett on an errand to the village. The weather was fine, and since the distance was scarcely more than a couple of miles, Brett decided to walk. Following his uncle's directions, he took a path over the moor which followed the line of an old abandoned rake, until he came to the lane which led into Stoney Middleton.

It was an incredibly steep lane, with white cottages on either hand, curving down into Middleton Dale. Brett jogged down it happily, hands in pockets and whistling. At the foot of the lane was an ancient hostelry with a weather beaten sign of a rather sickly looking Moon. Another lane joined here—the one which ran the length of the dale— and beyond it lay a stream and a tall mill. Beyond the mill again lay a cluster of cottages and the tower of the village church, all at valley level, but then the village climbed up the other side of the dale in a straggle of farms and cottages, half hidden by the wooded slopes.

Brett had been given explicit directions which he had no difficulty in following. At the Moon Inn he was to take the lane up the dale to the smelting house and then pass on his message to a Mr Hallam.

It was only when he walked up the dale that Brett realised the unique situation of the village. The dale became little more than a defile, hemmed in by tall limestone crags. On the northern side these were particularly imposing—frightening even, for they towered over the tiny cottages, which were cramped in between the rocks and the dusty road. Where there were no cottages, thickets of oaks surrounded the base of the rocks, which rose from them like the pinnacles and turrets of a white castle.

The smelting house was set at the top end of the village: a cluster of low pitched roofs and a tall square chimney belching sulphurous smoke.

Inside the smelting house it was dark, hot, and full of acrid fumes, so that Brett's eyes began to water and he was attacked by a fit of coughing. It was a minute or two before he recovered sufficiently to look about him. The scene was an astonishing one. Two men with long iron bars were poking and levering at a glowing furnace which cast out on them a fierce ruddy glow so that their bare torsos gleamed like burnished copper. At either side of the furnace were a pair of huge bellows, huffing and puffing alternately and driven by the trundling crash of a water wheel.

"Now then young 'un. What does tha want?" A tall man, grimy with sweat and dirt, had appeared from the shadows and stood in front of Brett. In his arms he carried a large iron dish.

"I'm seeking Mr Hallam to ask about Mr Booth's last batch," said Brett.

"Ah'm Hallam," the man said, turning away and walking towards the furnace. Brett followed. "Tha con tell Mester Booth that yon ore were noan of good quality."

2

He put the dish under the furnace workstone.

"Tha new to t'district?" Hallam asked.

"Yes. Mr Booth is my uncle. I'm staying with him awhile."

Hallam nodded comprehendingly, as though the whole complicated family tree of the Booths was an open book to him. "Tha's getten a look on Will Booth's sister," he said.

He had not taken his eyes off the brightly burning furnace for a second as he talked to Brett. "Aw reet —set her up lads," he ordered suddenly, "her's burnin' weel enough."

The two men began to pile up the furnace with coals and ore, and a mixture of cinders and half smelted lead ore which lay hotly on the workstone, a slab of rock in front of the fire. A shovelful of broken limestone and another of spar crystals went too, then the whole was hemmed in by a wall of peat turves. It was a skilful business but the men worked quickly before the heat of the fire died. When it was done, Hallam relaxed a little.

"No time for chattin' when we're setting-up," he explained. "But her'll burn for a bit now and t'lads'll watch for t'lead runnin' into t'pan."

They walked to the door and Brett was glad of the cool October air after the heat of the smelting house. Hallam was wiping his black, greasy hands on a sweat rag. He looked thoughtful.

"Yon ore we mentioned—Will Booth's—it came from t'Top Level, Whistling Clough?" He asked.

"Aye, sir, that is so," Brett replied.

"Pity. 'Twere a good level at one time were yon.

But her's finished now judging by aw accounts. Has
Will getten much lately?"

"I believe not," replied Brett.

" 'Twere a shame if Whistling Clough mine were
abandoned," said Hallam.

"Oh! But I doubt whether Uncle Will would
ever abandon the mine," cried Brett. "It's been in
the family for years."

Hallam gave a little smile. "Aye, lad, that much
ah'm aware on—tha cawn't teach thi granny to
suck eggs, tha knows!" Seeing Brett's puzzled look
he went on. "What ah means is this: Middleton
lives and breathes lead and lead minin', and
theer's noan a mon—nor boy nayther, come to
that—as doesn't know every Meare in t'Liberty:
who owns it an' for how long."

Brett's cheeks coloured. "I'm sorry, sir," he said.
"I meant no disrespect to your knowledge of your
craft—"

"Nay, nay, think nowt of it. Tha'rt a foreigner
after aw and knows nowt about lead. Tak Whistling
Clough, for instance: did tha know it were once one
o't'most prosperous mines i'Middleton? That's how
t'Booths made their brass!"

"All the more reason not to give it up," said Brett.

"Happen. But it's noan as simple as that. Barmester might have summat for t'say."

"Barmester? Who's he?"

"He's t'chap as looks after aw t'mines i't'Liberty
o' Eyam and Middleton. He sees that everyone
keeps to t'Code as set down by t'Coort."

"Ah! The Code," said Brett, remembering what

Abby had told him of the lead miners' special laws.

"Aye—and it says i' t'Code 'If any mine stands nine weeks unwrought t'Barmester shall give notice and Arrest it.' So tha sees how it is lad—if Will Booth gets nowt from Whistling Clough for nine weeks, he loses it for aw time!"

As Brett strolled down into the village again his agile mind tried to fit together all the bits of the puzzle which he had felt surrounded Whistling Clough from the very moment of his arrival there. What Hallam had told him was revealing, yet at the same time disconcerting.

That Whistling Clough Mine had once been prosperous accounted for the well-built farmhouse, with its comfortable fittings and general air of prosperity. Yet the mine was not a large one—Uncle Will and Seth managed to work it between them, so the ore must have been easy to get and of high quality. This latter was borne out by what Hallam had said.

Now, it seemed, things had taken a bad turn. The ore was of poor quality and hard to work. No wonder Uncle Will was worried! As if that were not enough, unless the mine *was* worked—and to the Barmaster's satisfaction—he would be dispossessed.

Brett shook his head in wonder. The more he heard about these lead-mining folk the less he understood their peculiar laws and customs. They seemed primitive, almost barbaric. To think that anyone could take a pick axe and just start digging in another man's field without so much as a by-your-leave, and that a mine which had been held by a family for over a hundred years could be taken away, without any compensation, if the owner failed to produce ore . . . Well it explained one thing—why Uncle Will was desperate enough to try mining the Bottom Level. If he wished to keep Whistling Clough, he had no other choice.

The fumes from the smelting house still lingered in Brett's throat, a nasty acrid taste which no amount of wayside spitting could remove. He was glad, then, to see the sign of the Moon Inn, for he had a few pence in his pocket and a mug of ale was just the remedy he needed.

The Moon was a neat place, low beamed, whitewashed and prosperous. Brett looked forward to his thirst-quenching drink and quickened his pace towards the doorway.

As he drew nearer, however, the quietness of the little inn was suddenly shattered by a tremendous roar, like a bull at bay, followed by the crashing of upturned furniture. Brett's eyes gleamed. A fight! A pub brawl! It reminded him of his recent student days at Warrington and his pulse quickened. He could no more avoid a brawl than he could fly. He hurried forward, a grin on his face.

He pushed open the door, and with a sixth sense flung himself sideways just in time to avoid a heavy pewter pot which came hurtling towards him. The room was dark and smoky and it took a moment or two for his eyes to accustom themselves, but he could see that the place was in chaotic turmoil. Benches and tables had been overturned, beer

mugs lay strewn about and their contents ran in
sloppy puddles over the flagged floors. At one end
there was a bar of sorts where the landlord cowered
behind his barrels. Two or three other men who
looked like miners, were pulled back, too, into the
dark alcoves of the room as if they were trying to
vanish.

The cause of all the turmoil was the heaving,
flailing mass of humanity in the centre of the floor.
Three young men, fashionably dressed in gaily
coloured clothes which were now torn and stained
beyond recall, were laying into a great hulk of a
miner. The miner roared and his assailants cursed,
and the four heaved, punched and kicked without
any thought of quarter on either side. Now and then
the big man would send one of the young dandies
reeling and yelping with pain, but with three of
them against him he was obviously outclassed.

Brett recognized the giant at once. It was Black
Jake o'Langsett.

The unfairness of the fight and the way in which
none of the bystanders went to Black Jake's help
made Brett have an instant sympathy with the
villain. When it came to a fight, his hands ruled his
head, and though it was no concern of his, and he
had no knowledge of who was in the right or what
the fight was about, Brett immediately pitched into
the battle.

Black Jake had hauled himself to his feet and was
backed up against the bar, defending himself with a
heavy stool. When he caught sight of Brett his eyes
showed a momentary flicker of apprehension, as

though he thought he had another enemy to contend with, but when Brett butted one of the dandies in the stomach, sending him crashing into a corner, Jake's villainous face broke into a grin.

There was no time for words, however. The three dandies, though puzzled by Brett's sudden arrival, were in no mood to call off the fight. Fists and riding boots flailing, they surged into the attack again.

Brett had never known a fight so vicious. He used every trick he knew to defend himself and hammer his opponents. "Get-the-one-in-blue," gasped Black Jake, as momentarily they came together.

Brett had already realised that the tall young dandy in pale blue jacket and breeches, with a fancy striped yellow waistcoat, was the leader of their three assailants. Though slim of build, with an aristocratic hauteur on his countenance, he fought with a viciousness which Brett found almost un-believable. The man's eyes were black diamonds of hate, and it was as though he could will that hate into supernatural savagery.

Brett had no choice in the matter as events turned out. The man in the blue suit came at him with an empty wine bottle, snatched from a table. He lunged forward to smash it on to Brett's head, but a fraction too soon. Brett ducked and twisted sideways so that the bottle scythed past his shoulder. His adversary, thrown off balance by his own momen-tum, pitched forwards and at that same moment Brett brought up his right knee into the pit of the

man's stomach. With a wailing gasp his opponent
went down in a crumpled heap.

The other two, seeing their leader defeated, broke
free from the grasp of Black Jake, who was trying to
bang their heads together, and ran for it. The fight
was over.

Brett leant against the bar and took deep breaths.
He wiped his hand across his mouth and was
surprised to find a smear of blood. Now he wanted
his drink more than ever.

But to his surprise Black Jake grabbed him
roughly by the arm and propelled him towards the
door.

"We mun get away from here, lad," the giant
urged, "An' reet quick—afore them two young
villains brings their cronies back to finish us. Quick
now!"

They staggered out into the daylight and up the
steep road towards the moor. Black Jake hurried
Brett forward, and from time to time looked back
anxiously to see whether they were being pursued.
Not until they had gone almost a mile did he allow
any relaxation of haste. Then suddenly, he sat down
on a grassy bank and heaved a sigh of relief.

He set about feeling his wounds, like some animal
trying to lick itself better. Not a word of thanks did
he offer Brett for his assistance, nor did he enquire
whether the lad had suffered much injury. Brett
felt indignation at the man's total unconcern about
what had happened.

"And what was all that about?" Brett demanded,
as Black Jake finally decided no bones were broken.

"I suppose you were caught stealing sheep again?"

"Nay. Th'art wrong theer," replied the giant. "Tho' ah mun say ah've had a few sheep fro' Nathan Calver i' mi time."

"Nathan Calver?"

"Yon chap i' t'blue suit were his son—Brigham Calver. A reet nasty bit o'work is young Brigham."

"But what was the fight *about*? I think I'm entitled to an explanation."

Black Jake rose to his feet and looked down at young Brett. His face was as craggy and villainous as ever, but his eyes showed an inner struggle, as though he had some secret which he could not tell.

"Th'art a reet good feighter, Brett, an' as ah towd thee afore, th'art a hard lad. Happen tha should know what yon feight were about—but tha joint in o' thi own free will. Nobody asked thi to feight."

"Of all the ungrateful—" Brett began hotly, springing to his feet. He glared up at Black Jake, who towered massively above him.

The villainous giant grinned. "Nah then! Doan't thee go startin' another feight!" he said with a chuckle. "Ah've had enough for one day. But theer's some things as is private, and what passed between me and Brigham Calver is *very* private. We disagreed o'er summat."

"Very well, if you wish to be secretive, so be it," replied Brett huffily. "But you'll fight alone in future."

"Ah generally does," said the giant simply. He paused then added. "Ah doan't want to be ungrateful—though ah've noan forgotten tha did ta

2*

hafe a guinea off me at pistol point—so ah'll gie thi some advice for thi Uncle Will. Whate'er happens doan't part wi' Whistling Clough."

And with that, he sprang over the bank, and before Brett had recovered from his surprise, Black Jake had disappeared amidst the criss-crossing dry limestone walls of Middleton Moor.

CHAPTER THREE

Bottom Level

BANKS OF AUTUMN mist hung in the early morning light, as Uncle Will and Brett made their way along the track which edged the stream in Whistling Clough.

Brett's uncle had not been pleased with him when he had arrived home on the previous day. He had not been pleased on two accounts: first, the news from the smelting house that the ore was poor quality had sadly confirmed something he already knew but was trying to push to the back of his mind —that the Whistling Clough mine was 'closing in'; running out of ore. Secondly, he had been displeased at Brett's involvement in a fight at the tavern. That Brett should have helped to defend Black Jake was beyond his comprehension.

"Yon scoundrel is an out and out villain!" he declared. "Ah'd as soon defend a mad bull as yon mon."

"But t'was three to one, Uncle Will," argued Brett.

"Happen it were—but dost tha think Black Jake would hev come to *thy* aid if it t'were t'other road round? And who were these chaps as tha was feightin'?"

"Two of them I cannot say, but the chief rogue was called Brigham Calver."

Uncle Will opened his eyes wide. "Nathan Calver's lad?" he exclaimed. "Lord preserve us! Tha must be reet out o' thi yead to tangle wi yon folk!" But Brett was sharp enough to detect a change in the old man's voice, as though the anger had gone out of it, and the protest carried on just for appearance's sake.

Later, Abby told him that her father questioned her closely about the fight, knowing she would have learned the details from Brett, and on hearing how Brigham Calver had been beaten he seemed mighty pleased.

They walked into a clearing morning. The mists rose and vanished like the spirits of the night and the Derbyshire sky became a pale blue arc. Only the great moor remained sombre, as though it had been witness to too much tragedy ever to change its mood of melancholy. Or perhaps it was bleeding to death, thought Brett, punctured by a thousand old wounds where mines had for centuries attacked its bowels. The scars were plain to see, everywhere one looked.

"Owd Mon," said Uncle Will, seeing Brett's interest in the ancient workings. "Abandoned mines —some of 'em from the days o' Julius Caesar they do say. We caws 'em 'Owd Mon'."

"Old Man," mused Brett, aloud. " 'Tis a curious name for sure, sir."

"Aye, but lead minin' is a curious business. Nah then!—what's aw yon?"

He pointed towards a knoll of the moor where a

group of men were busy marking out ground and erecting some wooden contraption. "Lord bless us! It looks like they're puttin' up a stowe." And before Brett could ask him any questions Will strode off in their direction. Brett followed, curious to know what it was all about.

When they arrived at the place they were greeted by the men, all of whom seemed to know Will Booth well. One was a tall, stern faced individual who reminded Brett of some of the Quakers he had crossed at Warrington Academy. He seemed a man of some authority, for he was taking no part in the work which was going on, but watching everything with a sharp practised eye.

"Nah then Barmester," said Uncle Will, "what's afoot?"

"Tha con see for thisel, Will," replied the Barmaster. "Jess Oliver has set up his stowe and claimed his meers."

"That's reet," said a small, ferret-faced miner, coming over to join them. "Stowe's is aw set and made according to custom—seven pieces o'timber and fastened wi' wooden pegs—tha'll find no iron nails in it."

"Ah'll tak a look, aw t'same," said the Barmaster.

They walked over to where a wooden framework resembling the windlass of a well sat incongruously on the turf. There had been no attempt to dig a hole, as Brett expected there might be, though sods had been cut away in the shape of a rough cross.

"Tha's cut thi cross—that gives thee three day's

grace onyroad," the Barmaster commented. He examined the windlass contraption. "No nails," he said. " 'Tis a proper claim."

"Wilt mark out a founder's meer?" asked Jess Oliver.

"Aye—52 yards."

"Tha'll need moor nor a meer afore tha finds lead in this place, Jess," Will said jovially. " 'Tis as bare as a babby's bottom."

"Happen," said the ferret-faced man.

"Then ah wish thee luck," said Will, and turned away with Brett at his heels.

"And what was all that about?" Brett demanded as they strode together over the moor.

"That were Jess Oliver ayther being very cunning or makkin a fool o'hiself. I'm noan sure which—yet."

"But that stowe, or whatever it's called?"

"He were layin' claim to a mine, as is his right. He cuts a cross in t'ground and that gies him three days to set up his stowe. He sets up his stowe—a sort of winching gear for lifting tubs of ore out o' t'shaft and that establishes his claim. But the stowe mun be according to custom, held together by wooden sprags—no nails nor bowts. Then he measures out a meer o'land—happen moor nor one meer, it's aw accordin' to circumstances—and he stakes it. 'Tis recorded in t'Barmester's book and i' three week's time he returns to see how Jess is gettin' along."

"And then?"

"Why he cuts a nick on t'spindle of yon stowe. Three weeks later he nicks it agen and at th'end o'nine weeks he nicks it yet a third time. If by then Jess has noan produced sufficient ore to fill t'Barmester's standard dish, then he is dispossessed and t'mine is freed."

"But if he does?"

"Then he's getten a lead mine—but, mark ye, he mon produce a dish o'ore at t'Barmester's command or he loses his mine."

Once again Brett considered the strange customs of the lead miners. They seemed too simple to be true, and yet, as his uncle had said, they had worked for as long as man could remember—a thousand years probably, in one form or another.

It seemed hard luck on a farmer that anyone could start digging up one of his fields without so much as a by-your-leave, but there was sense in it too. The King, who owned much of the Peak, and the great landowners, were entitled to a proportion of all the lead which was found—usually one thirteenth, the so called King's Dish—which brought them a steady income, and not only that, it ensured that the lead, and sometimes silver, which was so vital to the needs of England, was diligently sought and dug. There was, thought Brett, a method in the madness.

"To mine for lead is one thing, sir," Brett said, voicing a doubt, "but how to transport it, and how to dispose of waste—surely that is trespass?"

Will laughed. "Nay, lad. That were thowt on years ago. If tha claims a mine then tha con claim access to t'nearest road, access to t'nearest watter for buddling—that is, to wash t'ore, and land for thi bing or waste heap. Theer's nowt as hasn't been thowt on."

"And are there no arguments—no disagreements amongst the miners?"

Will laughed louder than ever. "There's ne'er anything else!" he declared. "Dispute is constant— but we hev a Barmote Court which settles disputes."

They came to a place where the stream divided into two on either side of a low knoll. A well-trodden path led up the slopes of the little hill to a hut and a primitive looking mine headgear. Wasteheaps surrounded the mine, spilling over and down the sides of the hill, as though some giant of a mole had been hard at work. Much of the waste seemed very old, covered by windblown dust in which coarse grasses had gained a precarious hold, mottling them green and brown.

Inside the little shack, which Will called his 'coe', there was a chaos of mining oddments, rough heavy tables, odd lengths of planking, bars of rusty iron, and in one corner a pile of crude ore.

"We stores it here betimes," explained Will. "Then me and owd Seth Holroyd carts it down to t'stream for washin' and breakin'. That's a job tha con tak on: it'll leave Seth and me free to work t'vein."

"Can't I go down the mine?" exclaimed Brett, in dismay.

His uncle laughed. "Ah'll tak thee down to show thee what it's like in theer—happen tha'll be glad to coom up agen!"

He was as good as his word. When he had selected a pick axe from the jumble of rubbish, and two tallow candles which he shoved into a pocket, Will led the way to the mineshaft.

Brett looked at the crude headgear which was scarcely any better than the stowe he had seen earlier. It was simply a wooden windlass like those found on some water wells, though stouter in construction. From the spindle a strong rope played into the depths. It seemed to Brett a primitive affair compared with some of the coal gin-pits he had seen in Lancashire, where horses were employed to work the cradles. He wondered whether they descended by this crude mechanism.

Will Booth, however, soon showed him that this was not so. The miner launched himself backwards over the stone parapet of the shaft and set his feet on iron rungs driven into the shaft wall.

"Follow me down these stemples, Brett, and mind how tha goes—they're slippy wi mud, and theer's a few missin' from time to time."

Brett looked at the oval, stone-walled shaft plunging down into darkness. How deep was it, he wondered? Fifty feet? More than that, for certain! A hundred? He could not tell—he only knew that the longer he hesitated the more difficult it would be to force himself over the edge.

He lowered himself over the parapet, feeling with his feet for the iron stemples. The smooth soles of his shoes slipped on the muddy iron but at last he managed to twist his foot so as to secure a firm grip and he began to descend. It was eerie—and like the sides of a well, the grey limestone wall of the shaft was running with damp and sprouted lichens and ferns from its crevices. A cool, damp breeze blew up the shaft and Brett wondered where this air could come from.

It probably took him no more than five minutes to descend the shaft, though it seemed to Brett an eternity. His uncle was waiting for him.

"This is Owd Mon," he said indicating a gallery which ran out from the shaft bottom. "It were worked out centuries ago. We mun follow it for a few yards and then go down a turn: that's another shaft and it'll tak us to t'Top Level. Mind now—t'floor slopes and it gets dark."

The gallery was well-constructed and though the mud floor sloped as his uncle had said, Brett found no difficulty in keeping his balance. The daylight which filtered down the first shaft became dimmer as they progressed further into the mine and if Will Booth had not stopped him, Brett would surely have stepped into the black yawning mouth of the turn.

This too was descended on the hateful slippery iron stemples. The difference now was that the descent was made in complete darkness: an all enveloping blackness which added to the sensation of unreality. Brett felt as though he was a disembodied spirit condemned forever to go climbing down through Outer Darkness.

Will was waiting at the bottom of the turn. He struck a flint and steel and lighted a candle which he handed to Brett. Then he lit another for himself and guided the way through a second long gallery. The candles flickered uncertainly in the ever-present breeze, throwing grotesque shadows on the damp walls.

At one point they came upon a short branch gallery. Will stopped for a moment as if contemplating something, then said, "Yon's the turn to t'Bottom Level," and then moved on. Brett noticed that this was where the moving air came from: once they had passed the entrance to it, the breeze died and the atmosphere became stuffy. He questioned his uncle as they slithered and staggered along the gallery.

"We're in luck wi yon," answered Will. "Theer's sufficient air coming up from t'Bottom Level to keep t'mine ventilated. We runs an air pipe—we caws it a fange—to t'further end o'Top Level from yon turn, though how fresh air gets into t'Bottom Level is a fair mystery."

Before long the sides of the gallery narrowed. A light showed up ahead, and Brett could discern a man, on his knees, picking away at the rock face. The man turned on hearing them approach. He had a thin face and scraggy neck, and was perhaps fifty years of age.

"How goes it Seth?" demanded Will Booth.

"Not good, Mester Booth," answered the miner. "It taks a week to earn a day's pay at this rate. T'vein is closing in for sure, 'tis full on calk and brown-henns."

Will Booth nodded solemnly as though accepting the inevitable. "Tha mun keep at it Seth: happen us'll strike a cross-vein," he said hopefully. "Tha

ne'er con tell. Ah'm away up top to show t'lad
t'dressings."

They fumbled their way back along the gallery,
up the turn and the shaft to the open air. As he
emerged from the shaft, Brett felt as though he had
been freed from some terrible prison; as though the
earth which Seth was busily hacking away was
antagonistic. Yet there was a strange fascination
about the mine, and Brett knew he would go
back . . .

In the meantime his uncle showed him how the
ore was crushed and then washed at the buddle (a
wooden frame with a tray into which the crushed
ore was placed and through which ran water from
the stream). The calk and other dross was carried
away by the water but the much heavier lead ore
sank to the bottom and was easily collected.

It did not take Brett very long to realise the truth
of Seth's words as he worked the buddle during the
next few days. In load after load, laboriously hoisted
up the shaft, there was ten times more dross than ore.
Sometimes, after the water had done its work, there
was scarcely a cupful of lead, and the ore pile grew
painfully slowly. Ignorant though he was of mining,
Brett knew that such meagre amounts were hardly
worth the taking, and that unless something
happened to turn the wheel of fortune, Whistling
Clough was a doomed mine.

It was on the third day that Will Booth made his
fateful decision. Brett knew that there was something
on his uncle's mind, for they had trudged up to the
mine without exchanging a word, and usually they

passed the time in idle gossip. When they reached
the shaft his uncle spoke for the first time.

"Ah wants thee to coom down today lad," he
said. "Ah'm gooin' for t'explore Bottom Level."

Brett's heart missed a beat. The Bottom Level! A
part of Whistling Clough which had not been
opened for fifty years, and one with a tragic past.
He remembered how Abby had pleaded with her
father not to open the Bottom Level, as though to do
so meant certain death. Brett shrugged: after all,
what do women-folk know of such matters? They
lived on old wives' tales and fairy stories. Only
Uncle Will could know whether the level was safe
or not, and the only way to find out was to go
there.

Nevertheless, Brett was disturbed to find that
Seth also took a poor view of the venture.

"Yon's a dangerous place," he said. "It's ne'er
been opened in fifty years, and theer's moor than one
Booth been kilt down theer."

"Ah knows that," said Will Booth, "else ah'd hev
opened it afore this but now 'tis th'only road left,
apart from abandonin' t'mine. Ah've made up my
mind and ah'm gooin' down."

"Then ah'd best come wi' thee," replied Seth.
"Doubtless ah've been in wusser places afore."

But Will would have none of this. "Ah knows tha
means well, Seth owd lad," he said affectionately,
"but theer's no denyin' theer's danger, and 'twere
best not shared. Ah'll go and explore and if it seems
aw reet, then tha con join me."

There was no arguing: Will was adamant that

the responsibility was his alone and he would not let anyone share it.

They gathered at the edge of the turn which plunged deep and dark to the Bottom Level. As a concession to safety Will had tied a hemp rope round his waist by which Brett and Seth were to hold him as he descended, for the stemples had not been used for many years and there was no knowing how rotten they might be. The breeze came up the shaft and made the candles flicker, adding to the unreality of the scene.

It seemed to take ages for Will to descend the turn but at last the rope went slack and Brett tied it off on the top stemple. Now they could only wait and hope.

Will was gone for perhaps half an hour, and just as Brett was beginning to feel anxious, the rope jerked, indicating that his uncle had returned to the bottom of the turn and wished to come up. Seth and Brett hauled away, and a few minutes later Will emerged looking flushed and victorious.

He could scarcely contain himself. Thrusting a hand into his pocket he brought out a shining black lump of rock which he handed triumphantly to Seth.

"And what dust think on *that*?" he demanded. Seth examined it under the candle light and his craggy face wrinkled with pleasure. "Ah've ne'er seen a lump of ore like this afore, though ah've heerd tell on 'em," he said, his voice full of wonder. "Why! Theer's moor lead i' this single piece than ah've been winnin' i' two hours' hard work!"

"Aye, and theer's plenty moor wheer yon came from," cried Will enthusiastically.

"Howd on a bit, Mester Booth," warned Seth, his miner's natural caution coming to the fore. "Men such as thi fayther and his fayther didn't leave ore like yon if it were simple to get howd on it!"

"Tha speaks no moor than t'truth," replied Will, "but ah reckons they were afraid o't'woughs. They're collapsed i'places and are fair rotten aw towd, but wi' strong wallin' they could be made safe enough."

Seth shook his head dubiously. To have galleries where the sides were composed of rotten rock was no light matter: it was all too easy for rock falls to take place, perhaps entombing the miners.

"Ony road, ah'm gooin' down agen," said Will. "Theer's a blockage at t'far end as wants shiftin'. Aw it needs is a few blows wi a pick." He took his candle and went in search of the necessary tool.

"Is it really dangerous, Seth?" Brett asked.

"Mebbe—'tis hard for t'tell when t'woughs are rotten."

Will Booth returned with a pick and shovel which he proceeded to lower down the turn on the rope. He himself dispensed with its aid since the stemples were apparently still sound. "Expect me back in hafe an hour," he said, and disappeared once again into the dark yawning hole which led to the Bottom Level.

From time to time Seth and Brett could hear the muffled clack of pick on rock as Will worked at the blockage. Their own anxiety had abated; the passage of time, with Will still safe, had dispelled their fears of the Bottom Level. Seth became quite optimistic—the quality of ore was excellent, and the Bottom Level could be worth a fortune, he declared.

Suddenly there was a sharp crack like a whip lash and a rumble like distant guns. The earth tremored and a blast of air whistled up the turn; snuffing out two of the three candles. Both men sprang to their feet in alarm.

"My God!" cried Seth. "A faw! A rock faw—t'mester's trapped for certain."

Brett threw himself on the ground and shouted down the black hole. "Uncle Will! Uncle Will!"—his voice edged with desperation.

"Will—Will—Will—" echoed the empty shaft.

"I'm going down," Brett cried. "He may need help."

"Tha'll get thisel kilt!" objected Seth. "It con faw agen."

"I've got to try," Brett said grimly. He examined the rope, an idea forming in his mind.

"I'm going down on the rope, 'tis quicker."

With as much haste as his nervously fumbling fingers could manage, Brett tied the rope once again to the top stemple. It seemed secure enough—he only hoped that the stemple was not rusted and that the rope was a strong one.

For a few feet he climbed down the stemples, then grasping the rope tightly, swung out into the black abyss. The rope held. As quickly as he could, he slid down the hemp, gritting his teeth as the cord burnt into his palms. Within seconds, it seemed, he was at the bottom of the turn.

At once he had an unpleasant surprise. The

floor of the Bottom Level was ankle deep in water.

From his pocket he drew flint and tinder and feverishly struck a light for his candle. The scene which greeted him, imperfectly illuminated though it was by the flickering yellow flame, drew from him a gasp of awe. The Bottom Level was altogether bigger than the Upper Level and had been shaped with considerable skill and care. There were limestone walls, with mortar and timber shoring of the stoutest kind. It was obvious that when the Bottom Level was in production in the old days, Whistling Clough was a prosperous mine.

The water was rising, slowly but perceptibly, and Brett waded forwards into the gallery, calling his uncle's name. At last he heard an answering cry and hurrying forward he found his uncle pinned by the legs beneath a chaos of boulders. The water was already lapping round his uncle's face.

"Good lad, Brett," gasped Will, his face drawn with pain. "Ah knowed tha'd coom—but watch thi step, aw yon wough's rotted to Hell." He groaned, as though speaking was too much.

Brett set to work with his bare hands on the tumbled rocks, tearing them down and throwing them into the further passage. He knew that unless he could free his uncle quickly, Will Booth would drown. The water seemed to be rising more rapidly every minute.

At one point his heart leapt as the roof gave a sudden creak, and flakes of rock peeled off the walls further down the passage, to land with a great splash in the flood waters.

At last, however, he could lift his uncle free from the debris and help him along the flooded gallery. Will Booth was in poor shape—his left leg certainly broken, thought Brett, and possibly other injuries not so easily seen. But the old man was as tough as leather: though he groaned from time to time and almost passed out from pain, he uttered no word of complaint.

By the time they reached the foot of the turn the water was waist deep and still rising. There was no hope of Will Booth climbing the stemples, and Brett thought desperately of ways to get him up the shaft. There seemed only one way—the rope. It was impossible for Seth to haul up the injured man on his own, but Brett thought that if he tied his uncle on the rope, then went up the stemples to join Seth in the hauling, they might manage it between them. It would need to be done swiftly though—or Will Booth would drown in the rapidly rising water.

He explained this to Will who was only semi-conscious and beyond caring. Quickly he tied his uncle on the rope then sprang for the line of iron stemples running up the shaft. Looking up he could see the dark shadow of Seth's face and the flickering glow of candlelight—at least he would not need to climb in total darkness.

He moved swiftly from stemple to stemple like an ape swinging up on frail branches. He made height rapidly, urged on by the knowledge that the water was still rising. At about two thirds of the way up he was well into his climb when, without warning, the stemple he grasped lurched sickeningly. For a moment Brett almost lost his balance, but quick reaction made him press into the wall, palms on the rough stone surface.

Thoughts of falling a hundred feet or more to the Bottom Level swam into his brain. He felt sick and dizzy and it took every ounce of self-will to control his feeling of black panic.

When the first shock wave of fear had ebbed, Brett again grasped the stemple. It was loose. Unused for half a century it had corroded from its fastening, and the weights it had borne already that day was sufficient to free it. With the slightest touch of his hand, the iron loop worked up and down, ready to fall at any moment.

Brett was in a dilemma. It was a long reach to the next stemple—too long—yet he could not stay where he was. For one thing his uncle would surely drown, and for another he could feel his foot already quivering and it would not be long before cramp caused him to fall to his death. He had to move and move quickly.

The pale light from the overhead candles showed that the wall of the shaft was of rough limestone blocks. These were lichen covered with age and damp, but between the blocks there were generous cracks where once there had been mortar. It was his only chance and Brett seized it immediately.

Fingering the cracks he slowly pulled himself up, his shoes scraping the walls for any hold they could find. The meanest incrustations served. Inch by inch he advanced until, after what seemed an eternity, he was within grasping distance of the next stemple.

For a split second he had doubts about trusting it. If one was rotten why not the next? There was nothing for it but to trust to luck, and so he grasped the iron loop and swung on it. The stemple held.

A few minutes later he was standing by Seth at the top of the turn fighting hard to recover his breath.

"That were a near do," commented the miner drily.

"Aye," gasped Brett, "but we must get Uncle Will up quickly now."

Together they pulled the rope and raised the semi-conscious man up the turn. Fortunately he was able to help himself from time to time by using the stemples as resting places, but it was hard work hauling and when Will finally appeared over the lip of the shaft, Brett was on the point of exhaustion.

Will Booth lay in the mud of the Top Level Gallery, past caring what became of him. Once, in the candlelight, he opened his eyes and caught sight of Seth's anxious face.

" 'Tis all o'er, Seth," he croaked. "Bottom Level's flooded. Whistling Clough is finished."

CHAPTER FOUR

A Visit to Eyam Edge

IT TOOK SIX strong miners four hours to get Will
Booth from Whistling Clough Mine to his home.
They had responded readily to a call for help from
Seth, who had hurried to neighbouring mines,
leaving Brett to look after his injured uncle. Carrying Will along the gallery and hoisting him up the
shaft to daylight had been a trying business, then
there was the making of a rough stretcher and the
final long carry down the moor to the house.

At first the womenfolk had taken it badly, for it
seemed certain that Will was to die, but when he
had been put to bed and Dr Denman of Stoney
Middleton had been sent for, things looked better.

Dr Denman pronounced a broken left leg, some
minor bruises, and a fever, but with the sort of iron
constitution possessed by Will Booth recovery was
certain. It was only when she was certain that her
father would live that Abby rounded on Brett,
blaming him for what had taken place.

"You should have prevented him from going into
that infernal place, sir!" she scolded, eyes blazing,
the red tints of her hair gleaming in the sunlight.
"You call yourself an educated man! Tcha! You

cannot see sense when 'tis thrust under your nose!"

"But what could I do?" pleaded Brett, tamely.

"*Do*? Do, sir? 'Tis not *my* place to advise a gentleman how to act in times of emergency. A *real* gentleman would know. I hold all this to be your fault entirely!"

"But that's not fair—" Brett protested, hotly.

"Nor would a real gentleman have stood by in cowardly fashion whilst a sick old man faced danger alone!"

"But your father was as strong as a horse until this happened!"

"Calling him names does not excuse you, either."

Brett was furious with her. Had any young man spoken to him as Abby had just done, he would have felled him with one blow. For a moment his wild, quick temper rose and he had half a mind to seize the wench, throw her over his knee and give her a good spanking, but he restrained himself. Instead he angrily cried "Women!" and flung out of the room. Not that he had the last word, for as he strode furiously out of the house and down the clough, a window was thrown open and Abby cried "Coward!" at the top of her voice.

Tired though he was from his adventures in the mine, he almost ran down the clough towards Stoney Middleton Dale. How could anybody be so unfair—so stupidly unfair—as Abigail Booth? The very thought of it made him mad and he felt like smashing something—anything—that came his way. And to think that he once thought her a comely wench! He must have been blind. She was stupid and arrogant.

And yet the sunlight glinted on her hair like fire on gold thread and her eyes were wide and frank, her lips generous. With a rare curse, Brett picked up a fallen stick and smashed it angrily over a limestone wall.

Brett felt as though he needed to be away from Whistling Clough whilst his mind was in such a turmoil. It was scarcely afternoon, and across the gulf of Middleton Dale he could see the pleasant green fields and the level uplands of Eyam. There, too, were the impressive chimneys and buildings of the big Eyam lead mines, including those owned by the Northern Mining Company. To Brett they seemed a mocking challenge: they seemed to say "look at *us* Brett Assheton—we are the *real* lead mines of today—not those dismal little holes like Whistling Clough."

He ran down the hillside into Middleton Dale and soon found the path which led to Eyam. It was a good track, cutting through a small limestone gorge where someone had taken the trouble to lay out a plantation of trees, which when fully grown would undoubtedly add to the beauty of the place. The track climbed steadily but within half a mile came out into a cluster of neat cottages which formed one end of Eyam village.

It was a straggling place, Brett discovered, strung along a wide village street which had some fine merchant's houses, an ancient hall and a church of hoary antiquity. That it was a prosperous place was at once apparent, and the thatched inn, The Bull's Head, which stood directly across the street from the church, seemed to be the focal point of this prosperity. Well dressed merchants stood outside the doors discussing the affairs of the day and others from time to time came and went, as if the inn was a place of business, as indeed it was, for these men were buyers and sellers of the precious lead, and where London merchants might use a coffee house for business, the merchants of Eyam and district used The Bull's Head.

Brett strolled into the inn, bought himself a tankard of ale and a pipe of tobacco, and settled himself in a corner to watch the comings and goings of the merchants.

He had not been seated long before a dapper man in neat blue broadcloth and freshly powdered wig came and sat next to him. He looked all of a bother and obviously relished his first long swig of ale.

"Better," he said with satisfaction. "Much better!" And he took another long pull from his tankard. He looked at Brett as though he'd known him all his life. "Fifteen guineas a fother, young sir, fifteen guineas a fother. 'Tis most unreasonable and I told him so, fifteen guineas, no less—what say you to that, sir?"

"Most unreasonable," agreed Brett, though he had not the faintest idea what his new-found companion was talking about.

"Quite so sir, quite so. I can see you are a man of the world. Your health sir!" And the little man downed the rest of his ale. He seemed disposed to talk.

"Name of White, sir, Richard White—lead merchant of Tideswell and Eyam."

"Brett Assheton at your service, sir," replied Brett. "Assheton? Assheton? Not local—'tis a Lancashire family is it not? Pendle way, I believe."

"We're a cadet branch, sir, but Lancashire still."

"Ah! Then you're not in lead. Thought I didn't know your face. Know everybody in lead: Jack Nodder, Bob Clay, Dick Bagshawe—know 'em all, sir. Rogues the lot of 'em."

A sudden thought struck Brett. "Do you know Nathan Calver?" he asked.

"Know him? Have I not just been complaining about him? 'Tis Nathan Calver who has tried to push up the price of lead to fifteen guineas a fother—and I ask you what profit is there in that?"

"It sounds expensive," agreed Brett, "but what pray is a fother?"

"Eh? Oh, about a ton give or take a bit. 'Tis about what a smelt mill will produce in a day."

"I see. But surely other mines will sell at less?"

"Oh aye, but there's the rub. These demmed Eyam mining companies are always at loggerheads one with another and the two largest—apart from Calver's Northern Mining Company—are tied up in litigation so complex that the Barmaster has arrested their mines. In plain language, young sir, they cannot sell their lead until they've settled their legal squabbles."

"I see," said Brett. "So the Northern Mining Company has a clear field."

3

"Precisely, sir, precisely. Apart from a few small ventures there is no competition and Nathan Calver has seized his opportunity to push up the price. The dealers are holding off for the moment: we can buy in the King's Field—that's Castleton or Wirksworth—but I doubt, sir, whether we can do without the Eyam lead. He has us, and he knows it, the scoundrel!"

"What of Middleton Moor?" asked Brett.

"Mostly Old Man," said the little dealer, "worked out years ago, and rumour has it that Whistling Clough has flooded this very day."

Bad news travels fast, thought Brett, but he acknowledged that this was indeed the case.

"Ah! Then 'tis probably the end of the Moor— though New Man will be set up from time to time I don't doubt. Lead miners are forever optimists, young sir, always expecting to strike a rich vein, though they seldom do. On Middleton Moor, for instance, there's many a man gone bankrupt looking for the Lost Vein."

"The Lost Vein?"

"Aye, 'tis an old wives' tale that the miners tell— though there's many as believes it. It concerns a rich vein on Middleton Moor which was reputed to have been worked centuries ago. But the vein was un- lucky, the story goes, and so many miners were killed in it that nobody would go near it and it was erased from the Barmaster's records. Its where- abouts were known only to one family—the Skid- more's of Eyam—who passed the secret down from father to son but swore never to plant their crosses on it. Then came the Plague of '66."

"I've heard tell of that," said Brett. "Of how the villagers of Eyam stayed in the village so as not to spread the disease to their neighbours."

"Aye, and only forty-three souls survived out of three hundred and fifty. Amongst the dead were the Skidmore family, and the secret of the vein died with them. Or so the story goes."

Brett remembered the new mine he had seen being set up on Middleton Moor and he wondered whether this had anything to do with the fabulous Lost Vein. Perhaps, for the merchant had said there were always plenty of folk ready to try their luck when there was a fortune in the wind.

Saying farewell to his informant, Brett strolled outside and made his way up a narrow lane, hedged by autumn tinted trees, towards the ridge-like skyline. There was evidence of mining on every side, much more compacted than on Middleton Moor, for here the high land was narrow and not as wild; indeed, it was mostly cultivated.

Old Man in the shape of long grass-speckled rakes of ancient workings and decayed mine shafts dotted the landscape, but here and there the old workings were overshadowed by the new, where the mining companies were setting about the business in a brusque and efficient manner. Grey limestone chimney-stacks, square and squat looking, belched smoke over well made hoists and trim outbuildings. What a contrast to his uncle's mine at Whistling Clough! Brett felt his heart sink at the sight of these modern mines. How could his uncle hope to compete with such well-organized mines? Perhaps it was all

to the good that Whistling Clough was drowned: at
least it would save his uncle the misery of seeing the
old mine slowly put to death by these fine new
monsters.

One mine in particular drew Brett's attention, for
it seemed the biggest and best of them all, and he
felt drawn towards it by fatal compulsion. Instinctively he knew that it belonged to the Calvers and
sure enough, cut into the lintel of a stone arch were
the words *Northern Mining Co.*

Beyond the arch rose a tall grey building, capped
by flagstones and quite windowless on the side
facing him. A chimney sprouted out of the ground
nearby, but the thing which intrigued Brett most
was the unearthly sound of slow regular thumping,
mingled with an eerie sighing and gasping, which
came from the place. It sounded as though the grim
building was a prison for Devils, all of whom were
toiling laboriously inside.

Brett was intrigued and not a little afraid, too,
but he made his way round the building to see
whether he could discover its purpose.

The other side was more remarkable still. A great
archway had been built into the upper floors, from
which projected one half of an enormous wooden
beam balanced at its mid point. The end of the beam
was decorated with an arc of wood, from which a
heavy chain hung down to disappear into a narrow
mine shaft. In concert with the thumping and
groanings the beam ponderously swung up and
down, now dragging the great chain out of the hole
then letting it sink back in.

With Compliments

REVIEW COPY

WHISTLING CLOUGH & THE DEVIL'S MILL

Walt Unsworth

H/B £7.95.   S/B £4.95.

FROM

CICERONE PRESS

2, POLICE SQUARE, MILNTHORPE, CUMBRIA, LA7 7PY
(TEL: 04482-2069)

Brett realised at once that he was looking at a fire-engine. He had heard of such things, invented some years ago by a man called Newcomen, and used for the draining of mines, but he had never seen one before, and it fascinated him.

The other end of the beam went into the building and there, Brett could just discern through the opening, it was connected to the fire-engine itself. He determined to see this modern marvel of science, and he quickly discovered a lower doorway at the side of the building. A lean young man, stripped to the waist, was busy shovelling coal into a hot furnace, whilst a boy of no more than six or seven years perched like a little monkey on some spars above him.

"Coom for t'see t'engine, hast?' enquired the stoker with a friendly smile. "Tha's welcome, young sir. 'Tis fust 'un on this field and theer's folk as cooms a good way for t'see it."

" 'Tis a Newcomen fire engine, is it not?" said Brett uncertainly, wondering at the gleaming pipes and rods.

"Aye, 'tis an aw. Her draws moor watter from t'mine than aw thi gin pumps put together."

Brett climbed a stone stairway above the furnace to the great beehive-like boiler. The young boy, a ragged urchin if ever there was, swung down from the spars to join him.

"Yon's t'biler," the urchin commented. "Her maks t'steam for t'drive t'engine. If her maks too much steam her'll blow up—though her's noan blowed up as yet." He sounded a trifle disappointed.

He pointed with a grubby fore-finger to a heavy iron barrel. "Yon's cawed t'cylinder and inside it theer's a dammed big piston. Steam drives it up, then watter comes in and cools t'steam down and her sinks."

"How does it do that?" Brett enquired, full of wonder at the intricate pipes and taps.

"Search me," said the urchin. "They says t'air presses it down again, but I cawn't figure it out at aw. 'Tis a mystery for sure—magic p'rhaps."

Slowly but surely, as regular as some old, old, grandfather clock, the heavy beam rose and sank to the beat of the huge piston.

Brett went down the steps again, his mind trying to grasp a wild hope which had sprung into it at the sight of the great engine. Supposing there was such an engine at Whistling Clough, might it not suck the Bottom Level dry and make it workable again?

"What is the cost of an engine such as this?" he enquired of the friendly stoker, but before the latter could reply another, more cultured voice said, "More than Will Booth could afford, take my word for it!"

Brett turned and saw a large man, florid of face, with enormously bushy eyebrows and a straight, rather long nose. His lips were thin, hard looking, and his eyes were expressionless, as though feelings of any kind were alien to them. He was dressed in a sober blue serge, well cut and handsome, his wig was immaculate and he carried a silver headed ebony cane. He had a chilling presence, like a messenger of doom, and Brett felt a sudden touch of fear.

"I do not have the honour, sir," Brett said, controlling his fears.

"My name is Nathan Calver, founder and principal shareholder of the Northern Mining Company."

"I am—," began Brett, but Calver rudely cut his words short.

"I am aware of your name," he said. "You are the fellow who aided that scoundrel Black Jake in an assault on my son Brigham the other day."

Brett bridled instantly. "That was a fair fight," he said hotly.

The other shrugged as though it was a matter of complete indifference to him. "Perhaps," he said. "It is of no consequence to me. My son is a natural bully, vicious, relentless and quite without scruples —I find him a most helpful business partner."

Brett was completely taken aback by this man's cold and calculated description of his own son, especially as it was perfectly obvious that Nathan Calver meant every word of it. Before Brett could think of a reply, the mine owner changed the subject.

"They tell me that the Bottom Level of Whistling Clough is flooded—is that true?"

Brett nodded.

"Ah! Then I see your interest in the fire-engine is not an idle one. However, such an engine costs a good deal of money: more than a thousand guineas for a new one and even at second hand, two hundred guineas—has Will Booth that kind of money to spare?"

"I know nothing of my uncle's finances, sir," said Brett stiffly.

"Maybe. However, I think Will Booth has *not* that much to spare. To imagine a steam-engine at Whistling Clough is a mere idle fancy. The mine is drowned, and as far as Will Booth is concerned, 'twill stay drowned!"

"With respect sir, that is a matter for my uncle— when he recovers his health."

Nathan Calver permitted himself a rare smile, his tight lips parting to show discoloured, uneven teeth.

"I think not," he said. "The mine is dead and cannot be worked. If it does not produce lead, then according to our ancient laws and customs, it ceases to exist. The fact that your uncle is a sick man does not bear on the matter at all. The Barmote Court will dispossess him, and the mine, such as it is, will be any man's for the taking."

This awful thought had not occured to Brett, but he realised that it was true enough. Unless the mine produced lead within a specified period then it was simply non-existant. That there might be a shaft and coes did not count: *lead* was what counted, and if there was no lead there was no mine. And if there was no mine, why, any Tom, Dick or Harry could come along and claim possession.

"But where's the advantage?" Brett murmured, thinking aloud. "If Uncle Will cannot work the mine, then how are others to succeed? If he is dispossessed, then Whistling Clough will become Old Man!"

"Not if one had a Newcomen engine," replied Calver. "A fire-engine would soon pump the mine dry. *I have such an engine.* Not three weeks ago I purchased second-hand an engine from a dead mine at Winster. It lies there now ready dismantled, until I say where it is to be erected."

Brett was staggered by the news. He had a sense that events were moving out of his grasp, that money and power were beginning to shape the future of Whistling Clough, and because of the mining laws, there was nothing that he or his uncle could do about it. Calver was like a wolf, waiting for a sickly lamb to drop by the wayside. A sense of anger and frustration welled inside him: a sense of injustice that his uncle should be cruelly dispossessed of his heritage through a chance of nature.

Then to Brett's surprise, Nathan Calver changed his tone. Instead of the harsh, matter of fact voice he had so far adopted he became all sweet reasonableness and light.

"The mining laws can be hard on a man," he said, echoing Brett's thoughts, "and I for one do not wish to do Will Booth an injustice. But the plain fact is that for some time the Northern Mining Company have sought a grove on Middleton Moor, and this is our opportunity to acquire one. Whistling Clough is a poor mine, by our standards, but 'twill suffice for the time being. For that reason I am prepared to *buy* the mine from Will Booth."

"Buy?" Brett was confused, "But when Uncle Will is dispossessed you can take it for nothing!"

"Aye, that is so, and because of it my price will not be a high one. But dispossession is not immediate—there is a time lapse—and I could use that time to set up my engine on the moor. If nothing

3*

else, it would forestall any rival claims." He paused
and looked at Brett keenly. "Your uncle would be
well advised to accept my offer. Tell him what we
have discussed and he will see the sense of it. If he is
agreeable, then I will call on him and settle the
financial details. I bid you good day, sir!"

Brett wandered back into Eyam in a daze. On the
face of it, Calver's offer was generous—and yet,
Brett had sense enough to realise that Calver was not
the sort of man to pay for something which he could
have for the taking. There was something behind it
all, though what it was he could not guess. One thing
was certain: all that talk about needing extra time
in which to erect a steam engine, and forestalling
possible rivals, was so much hot air. There were
other, more cogent reasons, Brett felt sure.

Quite apart from the question of buying the mine,
why should a prosperous company like the Northern
Mining Company want Whistling Clough at all?
Compared with the Eyam mines, Whistling Clough
was nothing. Calver had tried to play it down, had
explained it in terms which just did not make sense.
Why so anxious to acquire a grove on Middleton
Moor? And if they *were* that anxious then why not
set up a stowe on one of the Old Man sites—surely
that would be as good as Whistling Clough?
Whatever happens don't part with Whistling Clough,
Black Jake had said.

It did not make sense, but curiously enough it
lifted Brett's spirits. Despite the puzzle one thing
was clear—Nathan Calver desperately wanted
Whistling Clough. And that alone was sufficient to

make Brett quite determined that he should not have it.

The day was a fine one, though with a hint of autumn frost in the air, and Brett felt it would be a pity to return directly to Whistling Clough. For one thing he still wanted time to think, and for another, he was still confused in his mind about Abby. The very thought of her made him angry in a way he could not understand. So he walked past the lane to Eyam Dale, and struck out along a path which wandered vaguely in the direction of Stoney Middleton.

He remembered that this side of Middleton Dale was edged with stark white limestone cliffs, one of which resembled the turret of a fairy castle, and thinking that this would make a good vantage point from which to view the surrounding countryside, he sought it out. It did not take long to find. There were a few trees and then nothing—the trees and the land alike just dropped sheer away at his feet, and Brett found himself standing by a dizzy void looking down on to the village.

The fairy turret was on his right, standing out from the main line of cliffs and higher than them by a few feet. He picked his way gingerly across steep grass and rotting leaves and before long came to the narrow neck of rock which held the turret to the parent cliff. It looked so insecure that Brett was uncertain whether to try it, but the conquest of the fairy castle had somehow become fixed in his mind. He *had* to try it—and so he stepped on to the rattling limestone and strode boldly across.

It was much easier than it seemed. He found himself on a lumpy platform no more than a few square feet in area and sheer on all sides for a hundred feet or more. A sense of elation swept over him. Here, on this tiny islet in the sky, he was king: nobody, *nobody*, could take it from him either by force or money. Brett Assheton knew power for the first time, and he looked down pityingly on the tiny figures and toy houses of Stoney Middleton.

Then his gaze wandered across the dale to where the great humpy brown moor rose like a sleeping whale. He couldn't see Whistling Clough, but it was there, somewhere in that barren waste. It brought him back to reality. On the moor there were no fairy castles, no island kingdoms ruled by one man. There was only an infinite waste, where people played out their lives fighting and loving one another. That, and lead.

CHAPTER FIVE

The Treachery of Brigham Calver

WHEN BRETT RETURNED to Whistling Clough he found Abby not only willing to forgive him (though he had really nothing to be forgiven) but anxious for his welfare, he had been away so long. He got the idea that she half feared he had run away—back to Lancashire perhaps—and it made him strangely elated to know that she was anxious about his safety.

He told her about Eyam and his meeting with Nathan Calver, expecting her to be shocked at the man's effrontery, but Abby took the news calmly enough.

"We must try to stop him, of course—though I cannot see how it is to be managed," she said. "The plain fact is that he is in the right, whether we like it or no. If Whistling Clough becomes Old Man, then it is open for anybody to try to revive it. Mark this though, Cousin Brett—'tis a big chance that Calver will be taking, for if *he* fails to win a dish of lead inside the three nicks he too will be dispossessed and all Mr Newcomen's engines will not save him! He puts a lot of money at risk, for success is not certain."

"Aye!" growled Brett, thumping the table to

emphasise his feelings. "That's the part I cannot understand. Perhaps I know nothing of lead mining, Cousin, but I've seen a few villains like Nathan Calver before this, and they *never* take risks with their money. They only gamble when the stakes are high and the winning is certain."

"But how can that be?"

"I don't know—but I mean to find out. In the meantime I must tell your father about all this and of Calver's offer to buy the mine."

"Aye—now that is strange, I grant you," said Abby with a puzzled look. "Calver certainly seems in a hurry."

They went upstairs to the principal bedroom where they found Abby's father propped up in his massive bed, his head bandaged and with a deep purple bruise extending down the left side of his face. Dr Denman had assured them that his injuries, though extensive, were not too serious, but they would take time to heal properly.

"Joe Denman's a good sawbones," said Will, grinning at them. "He's a Justice as well, tha knows —so if he says ah'm noan for t'dee, ah reckons that's legal!" He laughed at his own joke, but the laughter hurt his chest and ended in a coughing fit.

"Now then, father, let's have no nonsense," said Abby, acting like a busy nurse and fluffing up his pillows. "You're a sick man and you'll stay here until you're well again."

"Oh-oh! Wearing pants are we?" said her father.

Abby flushed and said, "Father! Mind your language!"

He chuckled, "Well then, awreet—but who's t'mester i' Whistling Clough?"

"You are—and if you wish to remain so, then you had best stay abed and get better!"

"Happen tha reet, at that. Fact is, if 'twere not for young Brett here ah'd have been damped for sure."

Brett threw Abby a glance then said gallantly that he had only done what anyone would have done in the same circumstances.

"Well, mebbe—but theer's not mony as would have ventured into t'Bottom Level," said his uncle. "Her's flooded proper, ah reckons?"

Brett nodded.

"Then that's t'end of Whistling Clough mine. Top Level's worked out and now t'Bottom Level's drownt. It'll ne'er be worked agen."

"Others think differently," said Brett, and he went on to tell his uncle about Nathan Calver.

"I cannot fathom why Calver wants the mine," Brett said, at the end of the story.

His uncle shrugged. " 'Tis true enough that yon Northern Mining Company have wanted a foot-howd on Middleton Moor for some time," he observed. "But he's takkin' a risk wi' Whistling Clough. And tha says he wants for t'buy it afore ah'm dispossessed?"

"That's what he said, Uncle."

Will Booth looked thoughtful. " 'Tis a temptation and no mistake. Us'll lose t'mine onyroad. On t'other hond, yon mine has been in t'family for a long time—" He paused and looked at Brett keenly. "Ah'm gettin' an owd mon," he said. "Even if ah gets out o' this bed, happen ah'll not be able to dig for lead agen: Whistling Clough will be in thy charge Brett—if tha wants it. Tha mun decide—do we keep it or sell it?"

Brett was taken aback. In all his young life he had never had responsibility so rapidly thrust upon him, never had to make such an important decision. It was a minute or two before he could even think, then he saw his Uncle and Abby looking at him expectantly. What to do? Black Jake had warned him not to part with Whistling Clough whatever happened but commonsense urged him to sell, to get what he could for the mine. It was as good as lost already, so why not salvage what he could from the wreck? On the other hand he had a nagging doubt in his mind about Nathan Calver—what was the man after? What did he know that made Whistling Clough so attractive? The thought of Calver with his money simply brushing him out of the way made Brett's pulse quicken. Then he remembered the fairy castle of the Stoney Middleton cliffs: he remembered how proud he had been—a king indeed—and kings don't sell out.

"We'll keep it! Damn Calver and his money!"

"Brett!" cried Abby, shielding her ears.

Uncle Will smiled. "Aye lad, damn Calver and his brass. Bravely spoken!" He yawned. "Now ah'm hevvin' some sleep, ah'm tired. Tha'd best put thi thinkin' cap on: tha's work t'do."

"Work?"

"Aye. Tha's getten a flooded mine on thi honds. What art t'gooin' to do about it?"

Next morning Brett walked up the Clough to the mine. It looked exactly the same as the first time he saw it; there was no outward sign that it was dead and abandoned. He wondered how long it would stand, now that the forces which worked it had gone: how long before decay and nature reduced it to a derelict state, a mound of moss-flecked rubble for future generations to stare at and puzzle over.

There was plenty of evidence on the Moor: Old Man was common. Why did Calver not re-open one of these old pits? After all, there was nothing to stop him, and as far as Brett could see, one old pit was very much like another. Why pick on Whistling Clough?

Deep in thought he left the mine, and walked aimlessly over the short tufty turf of the Moor. What was it Black Jake had once said? Leave mining to the moles? The Moor looked as though it had been ravaged by giant moles: Old Man and New Man with their bing heaps thrown up into aimless piles everywhere.

He came to a shallow hollow in the hills, where a stream ran muddily southwards towards the Vale of Derwent. Here there was a lot of Old Man, following distinctive rakes, and a couple of working mines. They were small miserable affairs, obviously worked by families and by outward appearance not very prosperous.

Brett sat on a wall and watched them at work. Two boys, aged about twelve or thirteen were breaking the dark ore into small pieces with heavy hammers, whilst two women and several younger children, boys and girls, carried it down to the stream which had been dammed at this point to make a buddling pool.

The buddle was a shallow, stone flagged pit, about the size of a door, dug in the earth at the edge of the stream. The ore was thrown into this, and water from the little dam ran through a culvert into the buddle and out at the far end. Every so often one of the women would scoop out the washed ore and place it carefully in a pile.

It seemed to Brett that they were not gaining much lead. The pile of washed ore was pitifully small, and he wondered at the crudeness of the buddling process. He could see that a lot of lead—the smaller bits—must be washed away with the rubbish, and this was wasteful. Then he noticed that one of the youngsters would walk down to a pool in the stream, some ten or fifteen yards from the buddling place, and scoop up ore from its gravelly bed.

"Her gets washed away," he said, seeing Brett following him on one of his excursions, "but her comes to rest in t'fust deep pool her comes accrost."

He was a friendly little urchin, nine or ten years old, dressed only in shirt and ragged breeches, with bare feet, brown arms, and a face which was in-grained with the dirt of years.

"You don't seem to be winning much lead," Brett said, indicating the ore pile.

" 'T'aint a good mine, and that's for sure," agreed the urchin. "Ain't much left on t'moor ah'm a-thinkin'. 'Tis mostly on yon edge at Eyam."

Brett wandered away, deeper in thought than

ever. Was the Moor almost worked out? He couldn't
believe it: not that he knew much about lead, but he
could not imagine Calver setting up a steam engine
to pump Whistling Clough dry, if there was nothing
at the end of it. Nevertheless, the miserable condition of the urchin and his family made Brett
shudder; he hoped Whistling Clough, if he managed
to keep it, wouldn't turn out to be a poor mine like
that! He had no intention of descending to such a
level of privation, mine or no mine.

Brett followed the course of the stream, watching
how the water rilled over the pebbles and splashed
aimlessly at the larger stones, creaming over to one
side or the other in turbulent little eddies. He was
tired of the Moor, tired of thinking about Whistling
Clough and lead mining, and the stream seemed of
a like opinion, because it quickly left the upland and
tumbled into a deep sided dale where, sheltered
from the moorland winds, shrubs and trees grew in
profusion.

The dale was narrow, but a path appeared along-
side the stream, and both path and stream threaded
their way through the thick undergrowth.

Suddenly, two figures appeared on the path in
front of Brett. They were young boys—ten or twelve
years old, at a guess—and they sprang out from
behind the bushes, like monkeys. They were dirty,
dressed in rags, and each held in his hand a stout
stick.

"Stand and deliver!" cried the elder-looking of
the two, brandishing his stick.

Brett stood still, absolutely amazed. The boy who

was threatening him was all skin and bone, with a face drawn tight by hunger. He looked as though he had hardly the strength to lift his cudgel, let alone use it. His companion, smaller and younger, was in no better shape. Brett had no fear of either of them, they seemed more like two skinny rabbits than footpads. Nevertheless, he could sense the desperation in their wide and bulging eyes and it made him cautious.

"Well now, young sirs," he said, warily. "What is this about?"

"Your money or your life!" cried the younger boy, with such forced malice that he ended in a spasm of consumptive coughing.

Both boys spoke in a high pitched nasal accent that Brett had never heard before. Certainly they were not locals, for they did not have the broad dialect of the northern counties.

"As for money," Brett replied calmly, "I carry but a few pence, and as for my life I doubt your ability to take it. However, I must confess I ne'er did see such hungry looking highwaymen in all my life and I have in my kerchief some bread and cheese, to which you are welcome—when you throw away your cudgels."

The two young footpads were obviously perplexed at this. They glanced at one another, and the elder said, "We could bash him o'er the head and pinch his clothes—."

The little fellow looked doubtful. "He's *big*," he said dubiously. "Maybe he'd tan us—and then we're done for."

The other snorted. "You're soft! I wonder you had the courage to run away!"

Brett smiled. So that was it! Runaway 'prentices from one of the cotton mills. That was why he could not recognize their accent, for everyone knew that the cotton 'prentices came from the Poor Houses of London, and were sent into a terrible mill system that held them almost as slaves until they were twenty-one years of age. It was cheap labour for the mill owners, and the Poor Houses were only too glad to be rid of them, in order to save the cost of their food.

"Well, make up your minds," said Brett. "Do you want the bread and cheese, or not? If not, then we'll have a set-to, and I warrant I'll knock both of your pates together afore we're done!"

The little consumptive seemed quite put out at this. "He could too," he said to his companion. "He's *big*, I tells yer!"

The old boy was still truculent, though his courage was failing rapidly. "How do we know he won't turn us in for bounty money?" he said. "He'll get five bob apiece—t'aint to be sneezed at, Wilf."

"Nor bread and cheese ain't, either, mate," said little Wilf. "I don't reckon much to this highway-men game, anyway. We ain't eaten for hours."

Brett said, "Not to put too fine a point on it—you being gentlemen of the road, and all that—but high-way robbery is a topping matter—*quark*!" And he graphically jerked his thumb and fingers round his neck to illustrate his point.

"What's that to us?" demanded the older boy

sarcastically. "Life's cheap, mate—and if we don't die one way then it'll be another. Look at Wilf here he's got the cough ain't he? Wilf's as good as dead already!"

At this brutal truth the younger boy began to blubber, tears staining the dirt on his thin little face. "Don't go on so Jack," he sobbed. "You knows I hates it. Don't say fings like that, Jack. Not never."

"Oh, all right—but it's true all the same. Topping? Topping's clean and quick, mister. Why! I bet from the gallows, death looks good. Its life I hates— that's slow and painful."

Although Brett was no more sensitive to the cruelties of his times than anyone else, he could only feel pity for these two miserable wretches. And yet what they said was no more than the truth. Judging by their past, by the privation that had been their lot from birth, why should they look to the future? He felt in his copious side pocket and drew out a clean red kerchief in which was wrapped some dark rye bread and hard cheese. He threw it to the two youngsters.

"Here—take the bread and cheese. But I assure you that you need have no fear of me. I won't inform on you."

The sight of the food banished all pretence of villainy from the two boys. Ignoring Brett they threw down their cudgels and attacked the bread and cheese like wolves. They didn't even notice when Brett kicked the cudgels into the undergrowth.

He sat on a rock, watching them tearing at the food. What was to be done with them? He had given them his word that he would not hand them over to the authorities, yet in doing so he felt responsible for them. He could not let them try their foolish highwayman trick on someone else, or they would certainly come to grief. Brett could imagine the reaction of some tough miner if they tried to waylay him!

Suddenly, he had an idea. Why not let them stay in the coe at Whistling Clough mine? He could see that they received enough food to exist until such a time as he could think of a better plan.

"How would you like a job?" he asked, as they finished off the last morsels of cheese.

"What's that then?" asked Jack, the older boy.

"There's a mine I know needs someone to look after it. It has a small hut—not much, but a dry floor and roof, and you could hide there for as long as you wished. I would see you had enough food."

The two boys grinned, the first sign of real happiness they had shown. Not only were they agreeable to the idea, but anxious to fall in with Brett's plan. He felt something of a glow of pride that he had won their confidence.

"You had best hide in the woods here until nightfall," Brett advised. He explained to them how to find the mine, and where they could reach him if ever they were in trouble. Jack, the elder of the two, offered Brett a grubby hand.

"Fanks," he said simply. "You're the first *human* being we've come accrost."

And they disappeared into the undergrowth from whence they had sprung.

Brett followed the stream until the path wound away over a shoulder of hill and into Stoney Middleton. He was still not sure whether he had done right by aiding and abetting the two escaped apprentices. No doubt he could be in trouble if ever he were found out, but that sort of trouble rested easily on his broad shoulders. More to the point, the two rascals would probably steal whatever tools they could find in the coe and simply vanish with them. Somehow, he thought not; but when people are driven to desperation by poverty there is no limit to the crimes they will commit.

Stoney Middleton was basking in a bright autumnal sunshine which made even the white-washed hovels of the mine workers look attractive. Stools were out by the front doors and women sat gossiping and mending their menfolks' clothes, enjoying the last of the golden days before the vale sank into its long winter. Children played hop scotch in the dust and one little fellow, of four or five, trundled an iron hoop down the street, doubt-less pretending he was the driver of one of the crack four-in-hand express coaches.

Brett turned into the Moon Inn because he knew he was likely to find Brigham Calver there, and he was not mistaken. The young dandy sat with a couple of his cronies in one corner of the inn, drinking ale together and smoking long clay pipes, their elegantly shod feet propped on the table.

"By, mi faith," exclaimed Calver as Brett came to join them. " 'Tis the young bucko from Whistling Clough." The other two looked at the newcomer languidly, as though he was some specimen of animal life in which they had no interest whatever.

"Puts up a good fight," said one, as if Brett were not present.

"Uses his mitts to fine effect," conceded the other.

Brett was wary. He had no intention of engaging in another brawl with these three, and he did not want to lose his temper, even if they needled him. Much to his surprise however, it seemed as though the recent brawl in which he had helped Black Jake was not held against him. Quite the reverse: the three dandies seemed to hold him in respect for it, and Brigham Calver invited him to join them in a mug of ale.

"No hard feelings, my deah Brett," he said, flashing a charming smile. "A fight enlivens the monotony of existence in this dreary place, don't you think? Who wins or loses is of no account—'tis the spirit of the thing. Drink up, and have another!"

Brett sat on a stool facing Calver, studying him over the rim of his tankard. The young fop had about him an air of arrogance born partly of wealth, but also partly because he felt responsibility to nothing and no one. He would, Brett thought, have made a dashing cavalry officer: high spirited, brave to the point of recklessness, and a fine figure in a uniform, with a long aristocratic nose and contemptuous blue eyes. He would have treated his men like scum, no doubt, and they would have hated him—but they would have followed him to Hell and back.

Besides Brigham Calver his two companions were
of no account. They merely aped their leader in dress
and manner, but Calver aped nobody. He was
himself completely and that was dangerous, because his eyes were those of a man who knows himself to be superior to his fellows, and cold like those
of a reptile. There was nothing, thought Brett, that
this man would not do to have his own way.

Brett put down his tankard, carefully wiped his
lips and said. "I talked with your father yesterday.
It seems he would have Whistling Clough."

"Oh Lord! Dreary business," exclaimed Calver
in mock anguish, "How I do hate it!"

"I thought he might have apprised you of the
matter."

Calver sighed and said, "I believe he did mention
something of the sort."

"He offered my uncle money for the mine—
though 'twould seem he could have it for the taking
were he to wait a while."

"How like the old man—impetuous as ever, and
uncommon generous. Your uncle had best take the
offer."

Brett lifted his tankard and drank.

"What puzzles me, sir, is why your father should
want the mine. Perhaps you could enlighten me?"

The hard eyes didn't flicker. "I? Nay, young sir.
Not I. What my father does with his money is his
own affair. He does not confide in me his business
secrets—thank God! We are the perfect partnership
—he makes the money, and I spend it!"

His cronies rocked with laughter at this wit, and

Brett joined them. But he knew that Brigham Calver lied.

"Well then, I'll save you money that would be better spent on ale and 'baccy," said Brett lightly. "You might mention to your father that Whistling Clough is not for sale. We intend to mine it."

Brigham Calver smiled grimly. "Really? But I thought the mine was drowned and your uncle sick in his bed?"

"Trifling difficulties, easily overcome," lied Brett airily. "And as to my uncle's infirmity, why, he has made the mine over to me."

Just for a second there was a flash of fear in Calver's eyes, gone almost as soon as it appeared. Then his face broke into its most charming smile.

"Why then, lads!" he cried to his cronies. "Here's to Brett, the new master of Whistling Clough! We must drink to that!"

Despite Brett's protestations he was forced to join in the toasts. Success to Whistling Clough! Success to lead mining! Success to King George! The ale flowed quickly and never tasted so pleasant, and an hour later it was four very drunk young men that staggered out of The Moon, arm in arm, to go rolling up the road to Eyam, singing bawdy songs at the tops of their voices.

Brett hadn't a care in the world. The troubles of the Academy and Whistling Clough seemed trivialities when seen with sharp alcoholic reason. How he had misjudged Brigham Calver! Why, the fellow was the jolliest of boon companions! Curse the road up Eyam Dale! Why was it so steep? And why did

he feel so hot, and why couldn't the trees and sky
stay in their normal places instead of spinning
round and round and round. . . .

Plop! plip! plop! Brett opened his eyes, groaned at
the dull ache in his head and shut them again. *Plip,
plop!* Water. Somewhere there was water dripping.
He opened his eyes again and for a moment thought
he had gone blind. A mild panic seized him—he had
heard old sailors tell stories of men who went blind
through drinking cheap spirits—had he gone blind
through drinking bad ale? He could vaguely
remember The Moon and a lot of ale, and Brigham
Calver and singing. But the ale at The Moon was
good ale, or he would not have drunk so much!

Nevertheless, he could not see. Was it night? No
night was ever so dark as this was. His mind was
confused and his head ached abominably so that it
was several minutes before he realised the truth. He
was underground.

He staggered to his feet, groping at the invisible
slimy wet walls of his prison. Either it was an old
mine shaft or a natural cavern—he could not tell—
and how he came to be there was a mystery. One
thing was for sure—if there was a way in there was
also a way out, and he did not relish the idea of
staying in such a dark dripping hole for long.

But with his returning senses came caution. Which
way to go? If he walked the wrong way then he
could be going deeper into the bowels of the earth
and he had heard tell that these subterranean
courses ran for miles; Derbyshire was riddled with

them, the county was hollow like a drum, and once entrapped a man might never see daylight again.

On the other hand if it was a mine there was the danger of stepping into an open turn, plunging to his death.

Brett shuddered and slumped down again. Trapped! A wave of bitter anger and remorse swept over him like a tidal wave. Tears welled to his eyes and he beat his fists impotently on the wet floor. Fool! Fool! Fool! With him out of the way what was to stop Uncle Will from losing Whistling Clough? He should have suspected a trap. Common sense had warned him that Brigham Calver would stop at nothing.

CHAPTER SIX

The Boggart of Whistling Clough

IT WAS SEVERAL minutes before Brett became aware of a slight current of air wafting gently across his cheeks. It stirred the recesses of his mind: there was a draught like this in Whistling Clough, he remembered. Could it be that the air was filtering in by some opening from the outside world?

He staggered to his feet. It was worth a try. Perhaps the gentle breeze would direct him to a way out of his tomb. If not, then too bad—but anything was better than just sitting in the oppressive darkness.

Facing into the air current, Brett began to edge his way along the dark passage, using the rough walls as his guide. He stepped carefully, feeling every foot of the way before trusting to go forward, in case he should step into nothingness and go pitching down a shaft to certain death. If only he could see!

It was a slow, nerve-racking business. Once or twice he thought he had come to a dead end, only to discover that the passage turned at an angle, or that there was a blockage to be negotiated. The danger cleared his fuddled head, making his senses razor sharp. Nowhere did his groping fingers touch upon wood shoring, and the walls were so uneven that it seemed impossible that they were man made. The further he advanced the more convinced he became that he was in a natural cave system.

After half an hour or more, he was stopped by an obstacle which seemed insurmountable. The gallery he was in ended abruptly in a blank wall and though he searched with desperate fingers every inch of the blackness he could find no continuation of the passage. Sweat stood out on his brow and he felt a rising tide of panic. Had he taken a wrong turning, he wondered? Was he irretrievably lost? Perhaps Brigham Calver had sealed the cave with boulders to make sure he would not escape?

Yet the current of air was still quite distinct. It was coming from *somewhere*.

He found the hole completely by accident. Tired and despondent he had slumped to the floor, and putting out his hand to steady himself had found the hole. It wasn't so much a real hole as a kind of slot in the rock, at ground level and no more than eighteen inches high. The air blew through it quite strongly.

Brett rolled over on to his stomach and pushed his head and shoulders into the slot. To his relief and astonishment he could see that a pale filtered light, whose origins were indistinguishable, illuminated the slot from the far side. Brett tried to wriggle towards it, but found that he could scarcely move. The slot was too narrow.

For one horrible moment he thought he was stuck fast, because he could not withdraw from the hole, either, and once again a wave of panic beat against him. By sheer desperation he managed to wrench himself free from the rock's clammy grip, to sit panting with fear and exhaustion in the dark gallery.

Somehow or other he simply had to crawl through that slot! But how? His fear had subsided and he thought the problem over, coolly. At last he hit upon a plan which might just work.

He scrambled to his feet and began to undress. Off came his bulky jacket, his waistcoat and breeches and finally his shirt and necktie. His shoes and hose he did not remove because he thought they would not hinder his progress, but the rest of his clothes he made into a neat bundle and pushing them into the hole, squirmed his head and shoulders after them.

The bundle blocked the light so that he was not able to see as well as previously, but he was delighted to feel how much freer he was in the restricting slot. He pushed his bundle with his head and tried to wriggle forwards. This time he was successful: the extra inch or so gained by stripping naked made all the difference.

He advanced inch by inch, pausing every now and then for breath and wincing as the sharp rocks scratched at his shoulders and arms. It was sheer torture, like dragging one's body over a bed of nails, or a bramble patch, but it was the only way. It took Brett fifteen minutes to negotiate the slot: fifteen agonising minutes and when he finally pulled himself out at the far end, trickles of blood were running from the scratches and cuts on his body.

He found himself in a wonderful fairyland, the

like of which he had never imagined. He was standing on a gravel shore by the edge of a wide, black pool which stretched across the floor of a great chamber. The cavern soared up, until it reached into invisible black recesses, but at the sides, where it was lower, strange pillars of opalescent limestone ran from the roof into the pool. Some were only half formed, glittering teeth of rock in the jaws of the cavern. The walls too, held frozen cascades of the same substance, infinitely delicate in their tracery and shaded with incredible hues of pinks and purples. And throughout the whole, there was a gently filtered light, so that Brett imagined himself in the nave of some wonderful underground cathedral.

He dressed and set about finding a way out. He discovered that the light came from a hole in one side of the dome, through which cascaded a thin, spray-like waterfall. It was about twenty feet above the floor of the cave, and at the far side of the pool.

Without hesitation Brett waded into the dark mysterious waters of the pool and then, out of depth, struck boldly for the waterfall. The coldness of the pool almost took his breath away and his raw scraped flesh stung as though beaten by nettles, but Brett was past caring. It was make or break—either he clambered out through the hole in the roof, or he remained trapped forever.

There were plenty of holds and cracks in the limestone wall and he had no difficulty in pulling himself out of the pool. For a second or two he clung there, aching, wringing wet, with the spray of the

4

waterfall splashing down on his upturned face. Then slowly he began to climb. The rock was slippery and once or twice he almost fell off backwards into the pool, but he managed to climb on, forcing his way upwards against the cold splashing waterfall.

At last he grasped the edge of the hole and pulled himself up with a mighty heave.

He found himself standing not five yards from the road into Eyam Dale, where a passing carter, startled by Brett's sudden appearance from the bowels of the earth gave a shriek. "From ghosties and ghoulies the Good Lord deliver us!" he shouted fervently, and galloped off down the Dale in terror of his life.

Brett arrived home to find both Abby and Grandmother Booth almost besides themselves with concern. When they saw him—his face scratched, his clothes torn and damp—they didn't know whether to be relieved or more concerned still. As for Brett himself, he felt totally exhausted: the long walk up Whistling Clough had just about sapped what little energy he had left. He staggered into the house and collapsed on a settle.

Mrs Hallam was at once called to deal with this emergency. A briskly efficient housekeeper, she took one look at Brett and said, "Been feightin' again, hast?"

He shook his tousled head. "Not this time, Mrs Hallam."

"No matter. Us'll soon hev thee reet. Off wi' thi shirt!"

Brett sat up and removed his coat and shirt. Abby gave a little scream and even the phlegmatic Mrs Hallam pursed her lips when she saw the grazed and bloodied condition of Brett's body.

"Th'art a reet mess, an' no mistake," said the housekeeper, as she hurried out to fetch hot water and the home-made liniment which she guaranteed as a cure for all pains.

Grandmother Booth's face looked drawn and serious. " 'Tis gettin' too much," she said slowly. "Too much. Thi fayther hafe kilt and now Brett wounded. Yon mine is accursed!"

Brett shook his head. " 'Tis not the mine," he said, and he told them what had happened.

When they heard the story they were furious at Brigham Calver, and were for informing the Justices of what had happened but Brett would have none of it. "What evidence is there?" he demanded. "All I know is that I left The Moon with Calver and his cronies, then I must have passed out and when I came round I was in the cave. But how can I swear that Calver put me there? He will doubtless say that we parted the best of friends, he his way and me mine, and that he never saw me from that moment on. And he has two witnesses to bear him out, remember. As for the cave—why, he will deny all knowledge of it, arguing that in my bemused state I must have wandered in by accident. There's no proof, and that's a fact."

"You were lucky to escape," said Abby, tears in her eyes.

"Aye, though on reflection there must have been

another entrance, or they could never have gotten me in there in the first place."

Granny Booth nodded. " 'Tis all part of an old system," she said. "Natural caverns and ancient mine workings. 'Tis well known locally—but tha's had luck on thi side, for although theer's several ways in and out, 'tis a warren of a place and a mon could wander theer for days and ne'er escape."

"Enough o'thi argy-bargy!" cried Mrs Hallam, entering with a bowl of hot water and towels. "Let's be seein' thi wounds!"

And for the next half hour, Brett went through torture yet again as Mrs Hallam bathed and swathed his bruised body. Yet it was worth it. Within an hour, dressed in clean linen, he felt completely revived, and ready to do justice to the leg of mutton which waited his attention.

Next day he was up soon after dawn. The air was chill, and he put on a heavy greatcoat not only to warm his bones but because the capacious flap pockets would hold the provisions he intended to carry. Last night he had forgotten all about the two runaway apprentices he had sent to the coe at the mine, he had been so weary and exhausted. Now, after a good night's rest, he recalled their pinched, starved faces, and he was struck with remorse. Poor little devils! They were depending on him for their food, and they must be ravenous. He stuffed the pockets with bread and cheese, cold meat, and some apples from the larder. Fearing that Mrs Hallam might not approve of this raid on her provisions, he said nothing to anybody, but slipped out of the house quietly, and trudged his way up the path to the moor.

At first he thought the coe was deserted, but he realised that the two youngsters would be well hidden, out of harm's way. Even as he opened the door he knew that somewhere, inside, or maybe outside behind the bing heaps, four sharp little eyes were watching him.

"Wilf! Jack!" he called softly. " 'Tis me. I've brought some food."

"An' not afore time, mate," said a sharp voice behind him.

Brett turned to find the two waifs, axe helves held like cudgels.

"Aye, and for that I'm sorry. But after I left you I had a misfortune which delayed me. Still, I've brought enough to last a day or so." He brought out the food from his coat pockets and the two youngsters fell to eating at once.

Jack, the elder of the two, looked at Brett quizzically, in between knawing an apple and stuffing his mouth with mutton. "You had a flankin', mate?" he said, his mouth full.

"A flanking?"

"A thrashin', a beatin'—your face looks all cut about an' bruised, like."

Brett grinned. "In a way," he said. "Fact is I have an enemy and after I left you yesterday he tricked me into a desperate situation. I scarce escaped with my life."

"Garn!" exclaimed little Wilf, his eyes wide. "Tell us about it!"

"Maybe I will, one day—when I have my revenge."

Jack seemed pensive. At last he said, "This enemy of yourn. Is he a well made bloke, dressed like a nob—young feller?"

Brett was amazed. "How did you know?" he demanded.

"He was here last evenin'," said Jack, nonchalantly.

"Here? At Whistling Clough?"

"I never saw nobody," said little Wilf.

"You was asleep," said Jack. "You're allus asleep," he added.

"I still never saw nobody," said Wilf stoutly.

"Well, he was here I tells thee. 'Twere half dark and I couldn't swear to recognizing his face, but I'd recognize the cut of his rig anywheres. A dandy, that's what. I'd half a mind to waylay him with this axe handle, for he looked like rich pickin's—and you not having brung any food like."

Brett was horrified at the thought. "Thank God you didn't!" he exclaimed. "His father is one of the most influential men in the district, and he would have hunted you down and had you both strung up at the next Assizes!"

Jack grinned. "I doubts it," he said candidly. "They'd have thought it was your doing, mate—'specially as you say he's your sworn enemy!"

"Thank you very much," said Brett bitterly.

"Anytime, mate. Anyway I held my hand and laid low, 'cos he weren't alone. There was a big ugly brute of a bloke wiv him: a nasty bit o'work if ever I seed one."

"Black Jake o'Langsett!"

"Mebbe. But I'll not forget *him*, I can tell yer. Anyway, they prowled around a bit and talked in whispers and then they went away. Then I went to sleep—hungry."

Brett wondered what Brigham Calver and Black Jake could have wanted, and how it was that two men, apparently enemies, should be acting together. It worried him but there was little he could do about it.

"Lay low," he advised the two apprentices. "I will come again this evening and keep watch with you in the event of their return. I must find out what's afoot."

He returned to the house in time for breakfast. Abby was outside, feeding chickens, as he came striding down the track. She gave him a quizzical look but asked no questions, and for this he felt a warm affection because it demonstrated her trust in him. Mrs Hallam was less generous. Throughout the meal she made constant references to missing provisions, but Brett pretended to ignore her and she finally went off with a mighty "Humph!" and left him in peace.

After breakfast he went upstairs to see his uncle. Will Booth was propped up in his massive four poster bed with a bobbled night cap on his head, and a look of annoyance on his face.

"Damned wimmin!" he exclaimed, as Brett entered. "Won't let a man leave his bed even when he's well! If t'weren't for this brokken leg, ah'd show 'em who was t'mester i' this house!"

Brett laughed. Will Booth certainly looked healthy enough and it would not be long before he could move around on a crutch.

"And another thing," continued the patient, "it's too damned hot. They've getten t'fire hafe road up t'chimney. Oppen a window, lad, and let's hev a breath o'air offen t'moor."

Brett opened one of the leaded casement windows. The cool morning air from Middleton Moor wafted into the suffocatingly hot bedroom. He knew that open windows and fresh air were not good for sick people, or so the doctors said, but he could see that his uncle was uncomfortably hot in the stuffy room.

"That's a seet better!" exclaimed Will, as the cool air reached him. "Fust time ah've been able for t'breathe." His tone changed. "Ah hears tha's been hevin' trouble wi' t'Calvers o'er t'mine. Yon Brigham's a murderin' scoundrel and th'art lucky to be alive, lad."

"What puzzles me is their reason for wanting Whistling Clough. And the mystery deepens—" And he told his uncle about his two miserable apprentices and the visit of Calver and Black Jake to the mine.

"The Justices will be hard on thee, lad, if they hear tha's been helping runaway 'prentices," said Will. "But I sympathise wi thi compassion. 'Tis an evil system they've getten' in yon cotton mills, using little 'uns like slaves. And when they runs away they've nowheres to goo, and must needs resort to thievin' and villainy, or starve. As if we hadn't enough footpads and highwaymen, we must needs breed moor! But as for Calver and Black Jake, 'tis a mystery to be sure."

"I thought they were sworn enemies," said Brett.

"Folk like that are nayther enemies nor friends," said Will. "Brigham Calver will be friends wi' onybody he con use—until their usefulness is finished, and Black Jake o'Langsett is a rogue as will work for onybody who has money."

" 'Tis my intention to keep watch tonight to see whether they return."

"Then be mighty careful, lad. Tha'll not meet such another pair o'villains this side o'Derby!"

There was cloud scudding across a bright moon as Brett made his way up the clough towards the mine. It was a fine night but the autumn chill made him wrap his dark cloak tightly around him. It was ten o'clock, and he hoped that Calver and Black Jake had not forestalled him, but he thought not—whatever they were up to they would not wish to be seen, and they would leave it as late as possible.

At the coe, Jack and Wilf were waiting for him. "Nuffink happened yet, mate," reported Jack laconically. "Brung us any more grub?"

Brett handed them some bread and cheese, and they fell to as hungrily as ever. Wondering at the savage way they attacked the food, Brett reflected that the poor little devils had several years of catching up to do.

For nearly an hour nothing happened, and Brett spent the time listening to Jack's account of apprentice life in Litton Mill, from whence they came. He

4*

was horrified at what he heard, though he had half a mind not to believe it all. Young Wilf stood guard outside, protected from the cold by Brett's cloak. Suddenly, he slipped in through the door, as noiseless as a wraith. "Someone's a-comin'," he whispered, and slipped outside again.

Brett and Jack joined him, lying flat on a mound of old bing stones, where they could see into the clough. Sure enough a lantern was bobbing with the swinging stride of someone walking up the path. As it grew nearer, the watchers could discern the black outlines of two men, one of average height and the other tall and big. Even before the fitful moonlight revealed them fully, there was no doubt as to their identity.

They stopped by a rock in the clough, directly below the mine. Brigham Calver took from his pocket a folded sheet of paper which he carefully unwrapped and set beside the lantern.

"Ah sees no caw for these moonleet journeys," grumbled Black Jake. "T'cowd air from t'clough is enuff to gimme rheums."

"Rheum or no rheum, I need your knowledge," answered Brigham Calver testily. "And what's a few aches compared with a fortune!"

"Th'art reet enuff theer. One fifth share tha's promised—and ah'll howd thi to it. Between thee and me, young Calver, ah'd as soon trust a ferret as trust thee; but if tha tries to do me down in this, thee or thi fayther, by Hell! Black Jake'll mak thi pay for it!"

"The respect is mutual," snapped Calver

savagely. "D'ye think we'd employ a villainous, sheep-stealing drunkard like you, if we had a choice? But we need a man who knows the moors and its ways, and can tell lead when he sees it, and is not too particular how he earns his money. Thank your stars that you are that man—else we should see thee freeze in Hell first!"

It seemed to Brett that the two would come to blows at any moment, but their anger cooled and they began discussing the lantern-lit paper in low, earnest tones. As if to illustrate some point, Black Jake from time to time indicated a feature of the moonlit clough, and once scrambled half-way up the bank towards the coe as though seeking reassurance on a technical detail. To Brett and his two friends it was a mysterious performance, wholly without meaning.

Suddenly, little Wilf, exposed to the cold night air, gave one of his sharp consumptive coughs.

"What's that," Brigham Calver held up the lantern. "I thought I heard somebody."

"Ah towd thee t'were not good to coom here at neet," replied Black Jake, his voice full of superstition. "Theer's boggarts and evil spirits."

"That's old wives' talk!"

"Happen it is and happen it ain't. T'would depend on thi conscience, I reckons."

"Hold your tongue!" cried Calver, now frightened.

Brett's heart leapt wildly. The wicked demon that urged him to mad tricks came rushing into his brain. So Calver and Black Jake were frightened, were they? No wonder—since Calver thought that Brett's body was rotting in some dismal cave!

On an impulse he sprang to his feet and stood on top of the bing heap, arms extended, the moonlight casting its pallor over him as though he were made of sepulchral marble.

"Brigham Calver!" he cried in a ghostly voice.

"Calver! Calver!" echoed the lonely clough.

"Behold your doom!"

"Doom! Doom!" repeated the moor.

For an instant Calver and Black Jake stood petrified, gaping wide eyed at the ghostly figure. Then Calver gave an ear-piercing scream, turned and ran down the clough as fast as his legs could carry him. Black Jake just moaned with terror, backed away into the darkness, then he too ran crashing and stumbling down the steep track, towards Stoney Middleton and sanity.

"Gawd! I never seed blokes run so fast!" exclaimed Jack, once the villains had disappeared. "You frightened them good, mate."

"He frightened *me* too," whimpered little Wilf, shivering. "Cor—you looked 'orrible standin' up there in the moonlight. I do believe I've wet me breeches."

Brett laughed, wildly pleased with himself. "That'll teach 'em to meddle with Whistling Clough," he cried. "They'll not return in a hurry!"

"Unless they return for their lantern," said Jack.

"Lantern?" Brett had not noticed it. "You're right, Jack. We have their lantern and their paper! Let us go and look at our spoils of victory!"

Like charging savages the three of them jumped from the bing heap and ran helter skelter down the steep sides of the clough to the stone where the paper and lantern had been left.

Brett snatched up the paper and held it to the light. It was old and stained, and so tattered that it almost fell apart in his hands. The ink had gone brown, and in the faint candle glow was difficult to decipher, it was so faint, but Brett could make out lines and figures, calculations and instructions. What little he deciphered made his eyes open wide with surprise and excitement.

Suddenly he gave a whoop of joy which almost startled little Wilf into falling into the stream.

"This is it! This is it!" he yelled excitedly.

"What is what?" asked Jack, impatiently.

"This is why Calver wants Whistling Clough, my lads! Now I know their secret, and by God! I'll give 'em a run for their money!"

CHAPTER SEVEN

The Barmote Court

THE THURSDAY FOLLOWING Brett's escapade had been set aside for a meeting of the Great Barmote Court, and consequently Edward Morton, Barmaster of the Liberty of Eyam and Stoney Middleton had let it be known that all free miners should be present at The Moon Inn by two o'the clock, or give just cause as to why they could not attend.

For the village it was something of a fête day. Long before the appointed time miners had been arriving, meeting friends, and drinking ale at The Moon and The Grouse, a rival inn across the street. There were waggons and mules, laden with ore and ingots, horsemen who had ridden in from the more distant quarters of the Liberty, and even two or three carriages belonging to the great landlords. Bradshaw of Abney was there, and so was John Wright of Eyam; distinctive looking men in well-cut suits and carrying black silver-headed canes, who looked upon the general rabble and confusion with a lofty disdain as befitted men of their rank. There were some ladies too, though this was mostly a masculine affair, and making the most of the

occasion there were pedlars and chapmen, children
and dogs, all adding to the bustle and confusion of
an overcrowded village street.

Brett wondered how they would all find a place
in the inn when the serious business of the day
began, but then he realised that not one tenth of the
crowd had any intention of attending the court,
nor had any right to do so, since they were not free
miners. For them the Barmote Court was simply an
excuse for a holiday.

Brett pushed his way into the old inn, ordered a
mug of ale, and settled himself in a corner to await
events.

He had gone to the court smug in the knowledge
that he now knew what game the Calvers were
playing.

When he had captured the vital paper from
Brigham Calver, that night at Whistling Clough,
he had rushed madly back to the house, with Jack
and Wilf in wild pursuit, and wakened the entire
household. Mrs Hallam, who had opened the door
to them, almost fainted with fright at the sight of the
young ruffians all hot and out of breath, but then
her motherly instincts had asserted themselves and
she led Jack and Wilf away to the kitchen for a good
scrub in hot water (which they much resented and
cursed her roundly until she spanked their back-
sides, thus establishing a permanent friendly rela-
tionship) and a hot potato pie for which they
forgave her everything. Meanwhile Brett had gone
tearing upstairs to his uncle's bedroom, wakened
him, and with Abby and her grandmother looking

on, dressed in their nightgowns and wondering what all the fuss was about, he had proudly produced the captured paper.

At first Will Booth could not grasp the meaning of it all, especially as Brett's account of the night's doings was garbled and excited, to say the least. But when he managed to calm his nephew down, and took a closer look at the paper, he almost sprang from his bed, broken leg or no broken leg. He thumped Brett enthusiastically on the shoulders and hugged him, and Brett thumped him back in joy.

This was altogether too much for Granny Booth. "When tha's finished pummelling each other," she said with sarcasm, "happen tha'll be good enough to tell us what yon papper is aw about? 'Tain't Christian, waking folk up from their beds i't'middle o't'neet."

"Aye, tha reet," said Will, sobering down his excitement. "But this papper is summat that ony mon i' Stoney would gie his hand for. Its written by Skidmore of Eyam, dated 1666, and it tells i' detail about t'Lost Vein o'Middleton!"

Abby clapped her hands in joy, but old Mrs Booth was sceptical. "Humph!" she cried. "Is that aw? Ah thowt tha would hev moor sense, Will Booth, than believe i' such nonsense. Theer's moor good men gone bankrupt seekin' for t'lost vein than tha could count. Aye, an' they had bits o'papper an' aw! Fakes and forgeries meant for fools!"

Will was a little crestfallen, but not entirely put out. "Well this 'un looks genuine enough," he retorted. "An' we've nowt to lose. It says that t'Lost Vein connects wi' Whistling Clough."

"So that's why the Calvers were after Whistling Clough!" exclaimed Abby.

Brett nodded and said, "And why they were anxious to buy the mine. They wanted to be sure they were first—just in case someone else stepped in as soon as the mine became dispossessed. It's that which makes me believe in the paper. The Calvers are not fools—especially Nathan—he would not invest good money in a wild goose chase."

"I wonder how he came by the paper?" asked Abby.

"T'fact is we're noan out o't'wood yet," said Will seriously. "Theer's no chance o'gettin' a dish o'lead out o't'mine, and so by mineral law, ah'll be dispossessed for certain, probably at t'Great Court which is next week. Tha mun go to t'Court, Brett, and plead for an extension o'lease. 'Tis our only hope whilst we think on a road to re-oppen t'mine."

Brett was shaken from his thoughts by the entrance of Brigham Calver and his father. He lifted his hat to them in mock courtesy, but the older man ignored him and the younger gave him a look which would have withered an oak. They passed by, and found themselves a niche on the opposite side of the room. Black Jake o'Langsett was not with them, but then, he was not a free miner, and in any case, thought Brett, the Calvers would not wish to be seen in public with a man of Black Jake's reputation.

The Moon, already fairly full, became more crowded than ever as two o'clock drew near. The atmosphere was thick with blue tobacco smoke, and the ale flowed freely, but there was a quiet air of seriousness, unlike a normal ale house, as men talked in hushed voices as though appreciative of the occasion.

At two o'clock the great brass dish which was the Barmaster's measure, and a symbol of the Court, was solemnly hung from a hook in the beams. Edward Morton, tall and dignified as ever, took his seat at the end of the room, banged on a table with his gavel, and the Great Barmote Court of Eyam and Stoney Middleton began its hearing.

It started with the formal election of twenty free miners, known as the "Body of the Mine". These men were sworn to serve for six months (until the next Court) as a grand jury. Their job was to hear complaints, punish offenders, and generally see that the mining laws were kept. They came from a select company of older men, free miners who could show that they had a perfect knowledge of the laws and customs of the Liberty. They could certainly recite Manlove by heart; a sort of doggerel poem embodying the laws of mining, for though Manlove wrote about the district of Wirksworth, which was south of Stoney Middleton, the laws in both Liberties were very similar. The Body could make whatever slight alterations or adjustments were thought necessary from time to time, to enable the laws to operate fairly, but they could not alter the substance of them. The laws and customs of the mines were ancient, absolute, and next to the Ten Commandments, the most sacred laws of Derbyshire.

There was no dispute over the elected members; most of them had served before and all were well known to the assembled company. They accepted the honour with quiet dignity, and the Court then turned to other business.

Brett was impressed by the way the Court handled the various complex problems which were brought to its attention: justice, as the saying goes, was not only done but *seen* to be done. Sometimes the ruling seemed harsh in proportion to the offence, but there was never any complaint, for the offender knew what to expect if found guilty of a misdemeanour—the Code was absolute and unwavering.

If the decision of the Court was accepted without argument, the same could not be said for the presentation of evidence. Witnesses were brought to prove that both sides were right, many of them such obviously lying rogues bribed to play their parts, that Brett wondered why they bothered. More than once the whole room was in an uproar as witnesses and plaintiffs hurled abuse at one another at the tops of their voices, urged on by their friends and the general public. The Barmaster took it all with a detached calmness which came from years of experience, like a slightly bored mastiff watching pups fight one another. In the end there always seemed to be agreement amongst the jurors, who had an uncanny knack of ignoring the tissue of lying evidence and extracting the kernel of truth.

Besides the arguments settled between miner and miner, there were also a number of miscreants who had broken the inflexible code of the mining laws. These were judged to be much more serious: the room was hushed and the Barmaster, in a deep accusing voice called the name of the accused and stated his crime.

"William Mellor!"

"Present."

"William Mellor, th'art accused that on the 15th day o' July last tha didst sell a quantity of ore privately, wi'out the measuring o' the dish or t'Barmester's knowledge, and wi'out paying thi cope as by law th'art bound to do. What says thee?"

"Aye."

"Tha knows full well that what tha did was against aw custom and in defiance of Articles in t'Code. This Court upholds that Code, and will punish heavily aw those who transgress."

There was a tense silence as the Barmaster fixed the offender with a stern look for fully a minute.

"For not payin' thi cope," said the Barmaster finally, "t'court fines thi two pounds. For sellin' wi'out measure, it orders that tha forfeits five dishes of ore."

And William Mellor retired, a sadder and wiser man, wondering how he could pay the penalties. That he must pay them was certain, or he would be finished for ever as a free miner.

It was not until the more serious cases were dealt with that Brett heard his uncle's name called.

"Will Booth!"

Brett stood up, trembling slightly as all eyes turned upon him, but determined to save Whistling Clough if words could save it.

"May it please the Court, but I speak for my uncle who is sick in bed."

Edward Morton's stern features relaxed and he smiled encouragingly at the boy.

"Aye, lad," he said. "And tell thi uncle that we aw wish him speedy recovery."

"That I will, sir, and thankee. He gave me power to speak for him today."

"Very well—though theer's nowt much for t'say. By aw accounts t'Bottom Level o'Whistling Clough is drownt, is that so?"

"Aye, sir, 'tis flooded."

"And unworkable?"

"Aye, sir."

"And the Top Level is worked out. Is there a chance that t'mine con produce t'necessary dish of ore afore three nicks are cut—that is to say, within nine weeks?"

"I fear not sir."

"Then con we tak it that Whistling Clough is abandoned—that t'stowes will be removed and t'mine become Owd Mon?"

"No, sir!"

There was a murmur of excitement amongst the crowd. The Barmaster looked at Brett squarely and Brett looked back without flinching.

"This is Will Booth's wish?" asked the Barmaster, uncertainly.

"Aye, sir. He wishes to keep the mine."

"But con tha show good reason? Con tha gie me any proof that he con mak Whistling Clough work agen?"

Brett was tempted to tell him about the paper and the Lost Vein, but he held his tongue. Either he would be laughed at, or every miner in the room would make a mad rush for Middleton Moor in the hope of staking a claim. Whistling Clough would not be safe.

"We hope to work the mine again—as soon as possible," Brett said lamely.

Nathan Calver got to his feet. "We're all busy men here, Barmaster," he said, "and while none of us would deny Will Booth's hard luck and extend him our sympathy, the fact remains that the mine is flooded and unworkable. Whatever madcap schemes this boy might have, or whatever fond hopes his uncle cherishes, they cannot possibly work the mine again. It is the duty of the Court to declare the mine Old Man."

Brett wheeled on him, angrily. "So that you and that murdering son of yours can lay your thieving hands on it!" he shouted.

There was uproar at this. Brigham Calver, angry and red-faced, sprang up and would have attacked Brett had not some burly miners grabbed him and pushed him back in his seat. The Barmaster, too, was angry and called for order.

"That's enough!" he shouted, and when the room quietened he said. "Ah'll thank thee, Mester Calver, to remember who's t'Barmester here. It's for *me* to say what t'duty o'this Court is! And as for thee, young 'un, what dust tha mean by thi accusations?"

"I mean, sir, that the Calvers are anxious to work Whistling Clough themselves. They intend to pump it dry by means of one of Newcomen's atmospheric engines."

"Is this so, Mester Calver?"

Nathan Calver agreed, smoothly. "The Northern Mining Company feel that by using the most modern machines, and by a large expenditure of capital, Whistling Clough might be made profitable again. But such a venture is beyond the resources of Will Booth."

The Barmaster considered this. "Ah taks thi point," he said, " 'tis legal, though scarcely just. 'Tis like kicking a mon when he's down."

"With all respect, Barmaster, 'tis not so. We have offered to pay Will Booth compensation for the mine—though as you know we could have it for nothing once it is declared Old Man. Unfortunately, Booth has declined the offer—I fear he is under the influence of this boy, who is well known for his drunken behaviour and brawling in ale houses."

Morton turned to Brett. "And what dust tha say to that?" he asked. He looked very stern, but Brett could discern a twinkle in his eye, as though he was enjoying this fight between a young lad and the mighty Northern Mining Company.

"I can take my ale with any man, and fight as good as most!" said Brett stoutly. There was a cheer from the assembled miners, and a good deal of laughter too, and the Barmaster seemed to be having trouble keeping his face straight. "The fact is," continued Brett, "the Calvers have their own reasons for wanting Whistling Clough and will stop at nothing to get it. Ask Brigham Calver why he had me put away in a cavern so that I might rot till doomsday!"

"That's a lie!" shouted Brigham Calver, springing to his feet. "I know nought of his cavern or his damned mine. I do know that he once fainted in a dead drunk fit on the Eyam road, and that he was a companion of that well known scoundrel, Black Jake o'Langsett!"

There were murmurs of disapproval at this: it was obvious that Black Jake was not popular.

"As for that," Brett replied. "You yourself are known to keep Black Jake's company—paying strange night visits to Whistling Clough! You should be more careful—folks do say that ghosts haunt the mine!"

Brigham Calver went white with rage at this taunt but before he could reply the Barmaster said. "These are serious charges on both sides. Wheer is Black Jake? Con he be fetched?"

At once, Brigham Calver calmed down. "I'm afraid not," he said hurriedly. "The man's a well known rogue. Some friends of mine saw him stealing a sheep only yesterday and gave chase, hoping that at last they could bring him to justice, but the villain escaped. I doubt not that he will be far from here by now."

The Barmaster grunted. "Good riddance to bad rubbish," he said. Then he paused and added,

"Theer's moor to this case than meets the eye, and theer's an owd sayin': when tha not certain what for t'do, do nowt. I doubt that Will Booth con mak Whistling Clough work, but its been a Booth mine for generations and Will has ne'er broken t'Code. Aw t'same, he mun turn in a dish afore three nicks are made—but till then, he con keep Whistling Clough!"

This was greeted with general approval by the miners, but Nathan Calver, as unruffled as ever, called for a point of order.

"With respect, Barmaster, but how long is it since Will Booth presented his last dish?"

The Barmaster opened a ledger which lay in front of him and ran his finger down the columns until he found the entry he required. "Two weeks," he replied.

"Then the first nick is due next week," said Calver smoothly. "And Will Booth has just seven weeks in which to make the mine productive again!"

The Barmaster gave him a look of scorn. "Th'art a hard mon, Mester Calver," he said, "but th'art reet. Seven weeks it is!"

Seven weeks. The Council had concluded its business and Brett, unable to endure the smoky atmosphere of the inn any longer, wandered across the bridge towards the church of St Martins with its recently erected octagonal nave. It was a part of the village that Brett had not visited before: a little square, surrounded by cottages and the church, and boasting one of those strange petrifying wells which are so common in the limestone country.

Brett's mind was preoccupied with the problem of the mine. Seven weeks. What could a man do in seven weeks? He sat on the low wall and watched the slow drip of the water on to the objects hung there. How curious that the water should turn them to stone—yet there they were; old shoes and a tricorne hat suspended in the cavity of the well and already coated with limestone so that to touch them convinced one that they were indeed transmuted into stone.

It was strange, mused Brett, that Black Jake should run off at such an opportune moment. Had he and Brigham Calver fallen out after the loss of the paper that night? Perhaps to Calver the paper was no longer important—perhaps he knew all there was to know about the Lost Vein. Perhaps he had learned all that was needed from Black Jake and had no further use for him.

He watched the drops of water fall and splash on the old hat, each drop crusting it a little more. There had been that angry exchange between Calver and Black Jake. *I'd as soon trust a ferret*, Jake had said. Now Jake had gone—run away from the hangman's rope. And left unclaimed one fifth share in the Lost Vein?

Brett's lips tightened into a grim line as this last thought struck home. Surely not! A man like Black Jake who risks his neck regularly for the price of a sheep is not going to run away when there is a fortune at stake! *I'd as soon trust a ferret*—what if

Jake's premonitions had been right? What if Brigham Calver had done away with Black Jake, once his usefulness was outlived? It was certainly a possibility; Calver was unscrupulous enough for anything, and that story he told the Barmaster about Jake's running away had come just a little too plausibly.

The question was how? Black Jake was a big man, who could snap a fellow like Calver into two pieces with his bare hands. Shot? Unlikely. It took a sort of courage to shoot a man in cold blood, and Calver was not the type. That he would commit murder was apparent, but he would always make it look an accident.

The water dripped regularly, monotonously on to the hat. In a few weeks the hat would be unrecognizable, buried inside a tomb of limestone.

Brett sprang to his feet. Of course! *That was it.* That's how Calver could get rid of Black Jake—bury him alive in one of the caverns!

He almost ran the whole distance to Whistling Clough, for every minute lost might be vital to the saving of Black Jake's life. He arrived out of breath and red faced, and brushed aside all questions about the Barmote Court.

"Jack and Wilf," he demanded brusquely. "Where are they?"

"In the house, I believe," Abby replied, startled by his manner. "But why—"

But Brett had dashed inside to find the two apprentices. Much to his surprise he found them sitting on the floor by Granny Booth's chair being instructed in the art of reading. On seeing him enter, they sprang up, eager for news.

"What's afoot then, mate?" demanded Jack.

"Murder and villainy's afoot, that's what," cried Brett, "if we don't prevent it."

"We're with 'ee," Jack replied stoutly. "Is there to be fighting?"

"I think not—but there's danger for sure. Find rope and candles, aye, and a tinder box and follow me!"

In less than ten minutes the three of them were haring down the track again towards Middleton Dale. Brett was sure he knew where Black Jake was; certain that he would be in that same cavern where he himself had been trapped. The question was, for how long? Was Jake already past help?

Brett found the entrance to the cave readily enough. Beyond, as he knew, lay the waterfall, dropping twenty feet to the deep pool, but he had come prepared for this. Hitching the middle of the rope around a rock, he swung the two free ends down the waterfall.

"We'll shin down the rope," he announced. "T'ain't far, but there's a deep pool at the bottom. Can you swim?"

"Aye—but I ain't partickler fond of water," said little Wilf ruefully. " 'Specially dark water."

"There's nought to be afraid of," Brett reassured them. "Just follow me and keep the tinder box and candles dry!"

He lowered himself over the edge, the cold water splashing on his upturned face and running freely down his sleeves. Within seconds he was soaked through, but he went hand over hand down the rope until at last he was able to drop safely into the pool. Then he struck out for the dark shore, and was surprised how quickly he reached it.

Wilf came next, and Jack hard behind him. The two boys cursed the cold splash of the fall, but they were game and were soon standing by Brett's side. They lit the candles and looked around.

"Cor!" exclaimed Wilf. "Wot a hidin' place! A poor 'prentice'd be safe as houses in a hole like this." His voice reverberated round the chamber in hollow echoes. "Bit spooky though," he added, in a whisper.

"The chief difficulty lies ahead," said Brett, bending down to illuminate the small tunnel which led to the further galleries. "We've to squeeze through this tunnel—and 'tis a tight squeeze I assure you."

Little Wilf examined the hole and sniffed contemptuously. "Ain't nuffink to getting through there," he said. "Afore I was sent to the mill I used ter be a chimbley sweep, and I been in holes a lot smaller than wot that is. Let me go first—I'll be through in next ter no time at all, an' I'll let yer know what's afoot on the other side."

Brett agreed to this. "But take care," he warned. "There's all kinds of pitfalls in these caves. Watch how you go."

Wilf dropped to his knees and squirmed into the hole like a ferret after a rabbit. The other two were amazed how quickly he vanished into the tiny slot and more amazed still when only a minute or two later his voice came echoing through the tunnel announcing he had reached the other side.

"Can you see anything?" Brett shouted.

"There's a geezer 'ere, all bound and gagged. Trussed up like a chicken, he is, poor sod."

"A big man; an ugly fellow?"

"S'right. Looks like that geezer wot was wiv Calver."

"We're coming through!"

Brett stripped to his breeches and shirt and struggled into the hole, with Jack closely following. It proved easier going this way round but a tight struggle, for all that. It was ten minutes before they stood, gasping and panting, in the sombre gallery, fully illuminated by Wilf's candle. On the floor Brett could see the inert figure of Black Jake.

"He's dead," said little Wilf, prodding the body with his foot.

"Dead?" echoed Brett, a sinking feeling in the pit of his stomach.

"Dead drunk," explained Wilf. "Cor, mate, he don't half stink o'ale!"

And as if to confirm what Wilf had said, Black Jake let out an enormous, drunken snore.

CHAPTER EIGHT

The Sough

THEY REVIVED BLACK JAKE by throwing hatfuls of cold water into his ugly face. It is very doubtful whether his dirty skin had ever felt the touch of water before, so whether it was the coldness itself, or just plain shock which revived him, is hard to say, but after three or four dousings, he moaned and rolled up into a sitting position.

Though Brett had removed the gag from round his mouth, the huge man was still bound hand and foot and he struggled for a moment ineffectually to try to free himself, then he gave up and moaned some more.

"Mi yead!" he wailed. "Oh mi poor yead! This is Calver's doin', the treacherous swine. He must hev drugged th'ale."

Then for the first time he became aware of the three boys, peering at him in the flickering candle-light. At seeing Brett he gave a start. "Young Assheton, by God! Ah thowt thee were dead," he growled.

Brett thrust his face close to the giant's. "Then think again," he said angrily. "Though it's no thanks to you."

"I had nowt to do wi that," answered Black Jake. "That were Calver's doin'. Ah knew nowt about it until tha appeared like a boggart up at t'mine!"

"You ran fast enough!"

"Aye—and not ashamed to admit it. Yon moor is no place for decent folk at neet. Ah thowt tha were some evil spirit, appearin' like that in t'moonleet, and when Calver ran, then ah cut and ran too! 'Twere only later ah found out why Calver was so afeared."

His great craggy face broke into an evil looking grin and he continued, "Ah allus thowt as tha wert a hard lad, young Brett, and too sharp for a villain like Brigham Calver."

"That didn't stop you from plotting with him, you rogue!" retorted Brett.

Black Jake shrugged. "Aws fair i' luv and war," he said. "Calver seemed certain to win Whistling Clough, and I seed no reason why Black Jake should not hev a share on't."

"Even after he and his cronies had set about you at The Moon?"

"That were when Calver first tried for t'hire me," Jake replied. "He offered me money to help him wi his plan and we disagreed o'er how much. Came to blows, as tha well knows."

"I ought to have let him beat you senseless!" Brett cried.

"Happen—but tha interfered, and Mester Brigham thowt tha knew what was afoot. That was why he then offert me a fifth share in t'mine, and why he tried to do thee in."

"Of all the double dealing—!"

"Mebbe, but he needed someone who weren't a free miner but who knew t'mining business. Someone who weren't too partikler about t'law."

"Two villains together, in fact! I ought to leave you here to rot, you villain."

Black Jake grinned again, this time broader than before. "That's just what tha cawnt do," he said calmly. "For two very good reasons. Fust—we understands one another, us two—ah've getten a liking for thee, and tha's getten a sneakin' regard for me—don't deny it—because, young Brett, for aw thi fine clothes and schoolin' th'art a bit o' a villain thisel. And secondly, tha forgets that ah've surveyed Whistling Clough, and ah knows just wheer t'lost vein lies."

"Ah, but I've got the plans," said Brett smugly.

"Aye, ah thowt tha might hev. But how dust propose to use 'em? How dust propose to drain t'mine? Tell me that!"

Brett was silent. Black Jake had raised the crux of the matter. The fact remained that though he had the plans of the Lost Vein and though he retained control of the mine for a few weeks, he was no nearer to solving the problem of how to get at the rich ore.

Black Jake waited for a reply and receiving none he said, "Just as ah thowt—tha's no way of draining. *But I hev.*" His eyes twinkled in the candlelight. "Tha remembers what ah once towd thee about mi trade? Well, t'was true enough. Ah'm a sougher—a mon as plans and digs drainage tunnels i'mines and when ah were at Whistling Clough wi' Calver on

5

those two neets, ah could see straight off that 'twould only tak a short sough to drain it—no need for aw this fancy steam engine pumping! Though ah kept it to meself, and didn't tell Calver."

"Why, you double dyed villain!" exclaimed Brett in astonishment. "You were going to swindle Calver! As soon as Whistling Clough became Old Man, you could have staked out a claim on it and started your sough before Calver could assemble his engine!"

"Aye,—ah con see we thinks alike, thee and me, lad."

Brett's anger had vanished. He could see a way of hope at last. "Black Jake, you're the biggest rogue in Christendom," he said. "Here, Wilf lad—cut him free!"

Once Brett and Jack had recovered their clothes from the far side of the tunnel, Black Jake led the way out of the caves. He knew every twist and turn of the dark passages, which seemed to run for miles underground.

"Theer's caves and theer's owd mine workings," he explained, as he led the way. "They're aw of apiece. Ah reckons nobody knows wheer one ends and t'other begins. Aw this land is hollow, like a giant rabbit warren. But 'tis my business to know it, and 'tis not t'fust time ah've been down this hole."

They came out of an adit on to a green hillside directly overlooking Middleton Dale. Immediately below them a tall chimney belched sulphurous black fumes into the air.

"Why! We are directly above the smelting mill!" exclaimed Brett.

"Aye, and we can reach Whistling Clough, wi'out being seen."

That evening there was a council of war in the spacious dining room at Whistling Clough. At the head of the broad oak table sat Will Booth, propped about by cushions, his new crutches resting against the table. On his right sat Brett, his fine features bronzed now by the outdoor life he had been leading and his crisp dark hair curling down to his neckerchief, his eyes alight at the prospect of success. On Will's left was Black Jake, big and ugly as ever, completely out of place in the civilized surroundings of the house, dirty and unkempt, and a constant source of suspicion for Mrs Hallam, who thought he would walk away with the silver or murder them all in their beds. Young Jack and little Wilf also had their places, anxious to help. Brett had persuaded Mr Needham of Litton Mill to sell him the boys' indentures, thus freeing them, since when they regarded Brett as the next thing to God, their natural master, protector and friend, and whatever he said they regarded as law. Old Seth was there too, called up from the village by Abby, and sitting with his long miner's face expressionless, but missing nothing.

Abby, happy because Brett was so excited, hovered in the background, replenishing an occasional mug of ale for one or other of the menfolk, and listening to everything that went on. As for

Granny Booth, though she pretended the whole affair was 'stuff and nonsense' and sat apart from the others, by the fire, her hearing was such that she missed nothing either.

The paper Brett had captured lay on the table in front of Will, who summarised its contents so that everyone would know exactly what was afoot.

"Every mon here knows that t'Bottom Level has been a curse on t'Booth family for generations," he concluded. "Mi grandfayther, aye, and his fayther too, deed in yon pit, and but for young Brett here, ah'd hev like as followed 'em.

"But theer's one thing ah did discover: t'woughs are rotten, reet enough, but they could be held up by strong shorin' and proper wallin'. Every yard o' t'gallery mun need proppin'—and that's costly business. Happen that's why t'level were finally abandoned: wi'out proper shorin' it were too dangerous, and wi' it, well, game weren't worth t'candle. They still had t'Top vein.

"But theer's riches and riches, lads. Now we knows that t'Bottom Level con lead us to t'Lost Vein, why, we con afford to mak it as safe as houses!

"That is, provided us con drain it. That's wheer Jake cooms in—he reckons he con drive a sough."

"Ah knows Black Jake for t'rogue he is—and so does aw of Stoney," said Seth deliberately. "But this much ah will say—as a sougher theer's noan better."

"Ah thanks thee kindly for thi testimonial, friend," said Jake, grinning.

"The question is," said Will, "How long will it tak to drive t'sough?"

Black Jake ran his thick fingers through his tousled greasy hair as if pondering the matter. " 'T'would aw depend on t'nature o' t'rock," he explained. "Ah'm noan expecting great difficulties though—t'distance is short, and 'tis no moor than a simple adit into t'clough. My reckonin' would be two or three months."

"Two or three months!" exclaimed Brett in horror. "But we've only got the mine for seven weeks!"

"So tha said," Jake replied sombrely. "So we mun start reet away and work like Owd Nick hissel. Mebbe we'll do it, mebbe not—but we mun try!"

"Hast getten a plan?" Will asked.

"Fetch lead and paper, lass," said Black Jake to Abby, "And ah'll show thee what ah had in mind."

Paper and pencil were brought and Black Jake began to sketch out his ideas. This great hulking brute, this vagabond and sheep stealer, unwashed, unkempt and unwanted, moved his massive dirty paws over the clean white paper sheet, and produced the most delicate, intricate pencil drawings that any of them had ever seen. As he gently flicked the pencil to and fro, dreams became realities and what had seemed at the best a possible hope was drawn into a magical certainty. By the time Black Jake had finished even Granny Booth was convinced that the Whistling Clough sough was a practical proposition.

They began work a little after dawn on the following morning, when the first rime frost of the season had touched the moorland grass so that it crackled underfoot as they walked up towards the mine.

The first task was to clear the site of loose boulders and an old bing pile and then dig into the surface soil. Brett and Seth did the digging whilst Jack and little Wilf carried away the spoil in wicker baskets to dump it out of harm's way. Black Jake had calculated the spot to a precise degree according to the captured plans, but at first he lumbered about like a shaggy bear, on tenterhooks in case they were digging in the wrong place, checking and rechecking to see that nothing was wrong. As the day wore on, however, he became more settled, and he too, took a hand in the digging.

To Brett it seemed that they were an awful long way from the mine itself, but when he asked why they could not start from somewhere nearer, Black Jake explained that they needed the drop in the land in order to achieve their required depth.

"If us went too near we'd strike her too high," he said. "We mun strike at t'Bottom Level. It's noan so far."

The rubbish took a long time to clear and it was not until they struck bed rock that Brett began to feel excited again. At last they were getting to grips with it! The loose material which had hampered them and over which they had toiled for hours was gone and now there was only the limestone to tackle—hard rock, but the final barrier between them and a fortune!

But as he struck at the rock with his pick his enthusiasm soon vanished. It was so hard that he scarcely scratched it and he began to despair. Then he watched Seth at work: the old miner seemed to have an uncanny sense of the weaknesses in the limestone. First he would strike it in one place, then, for no apparent reason in another, and sure enough, a piece of rock would fall away as though it had been loose all the time.

Brett threw down his pick in disgust. Black Jake, who had been watching, took it up and with one blow brought out a piece of rock the size of a brick. " 'Tis a matter o'knowing where to hit it," he said. "Like when tha's feightin' wi thi fists—tha does better if tha knows wheer thi opponent is weakest. Me and Seth have lived wi this rock aw our lives and we know it—tha doesn't. Tha mun watch and learn and happen tha con tak a turn later."

As day followed day the new tunnel began to take shape. Some days it seemed as though they would win through to the mine in less than a month, so quickly did they progress, but on others the rock was so tough that they scarcely advanced a foot all day.

There was a lot of extra work to do as the tunnel lengthened. In places it needed shoring with timbers because Jake suspected some flaw in the roof, and like a true craftsman, he had the boys working at improving and smoothing the walls behind the main party to give the tunnel symmetry.

From time to time he found suitable crack lines which enabled him to 'burn off' the rock face. He would take small branches of greenwood and hammer them into the cracks, then light a fire in front of the rocks. The greenwood heated and the sap in it boiled and expanded in sharp violent explosions, shattering the rock and bringing down tons at a time. It was a dangerous proceeding in the narrow confines of the tunnel, but it saved hours of heart-breaking work with the pick.

As the tunnel began to grow and take shape, the tipping of the spoil began to scar the banks of Whistling Clough, an obvious landmark for curious eyes. Pack mules, too, laden with timber for shorings and sand for mortar were an everyday sight on the track to the mine, so it was not surprising that the whole district was soon aware of what was taking place. It became, in fact, a common topic for gossip, and though many people sympathised with Will Booth in his attempt to win back his mine, most regarded it as a lost cause. The sough became known as Booth's Folly.

Perhaps in the whole Liberty of Eyam and Stoney Middleton only two men took the project seriously, apart from the diggers themselves. Nathan and Brigham Calver took it very seriously indeed. In the elegantly furnished drawing room of their neat Georgian house, overlooking the church at Eyam, Brigham faced his father in impotent rage.

"Damn them!" he cried vehemently, striking his fists on his satin clad knees. "They have the luck of the Devil! I swear 'tis sorcery, no less. How else do you explain it?"

His father was taking things more calmly, though his eyes were cold and calculating. "There's no sorcery," he replied. "You underestimated Brett Assheton. He is much shrewder than you gave him credit for being. You have bungled this affair from start to finish."

"*I* have bungled——" cried Brigham, rising to his feet in rage.

"Sit down, sir, and don't presume to shout at me!" ordered his father, and Brigham did as he was bid. "The fact is you let your evil temper get the better of you too often—which is why we are in this sorry mess. Had you not tried to thrash Black Jake in the first place, none of this would have happened."

"You realise, I take it, that Black Jake must have been intending to swindle us all along?" his son demanded coldly. "That he must have been preparing for a sough from the beginning?"

His father shrugged. "What else do you expect from such a rogue? Of course he was preparing to do us down, just as we were preparing a similar fate for him, but you acted too hastily in that matter also. The time to dispose of the villain was once the mine was declared Old Man, and not a moment sooner."

"How was I to know that the Barmote Court would extend Will Booth's lease?"

"Common sense—but that's past history and does not help us to solve the immediate problem. I fear the sough may succeed."

"We could blow it up one night!" suggested Brigham eagerly.

His father gave him a look of withering contempt. "There you go again!" he cried impatiently. "You

5*

carry your brains in your fists, sir, instead of your pate. Why! If the sough was blown up, who would be the first suspects? We would! No. This calls for cunning."

"We could swear out a warrant for the arrest of Black Jake. He is a known sheep stealer and a notorious character throughout the district. A guinea here and a guinea there would bring us plenty of witnesses to swear his guilt before the Justices. With luck we could have him hanged after next Derby Assize."

His father smiled. "And with Jake out of the way, the sough could scarcely hope to succeed," he said. " 'Tis a pretty scheme, and 'twould seem you are not entirely without brains. But 'tis risky."

"How so?"

"Because we are known to be deeply involved in this affair. After the Barmote Court everyone knows we are interested in the Whistling Clough mine. In affairs like this, my son, you must assess the public mind—Will Booth has a lot of sympathy at the moment—a cripple fighting impossible odds—and though Black Jake is unpopular, if we have him arrested it will look as though we did it to spite Will Booth."

"What do we care about public sympathy, if we gain the mine?" snorted Brigham impatiently.

"We don't—but there are people who might well smell the plot and start to make enquiries of their own. Edward Morton, the Barmaster, is one—and the stakes are too high for such a risk. No. We must be more devious still. We must not take an active part. We must try to get someone else to stop the digging of the sough!"

Brigham Calver looked at his father. Their eyes met and held for a moment. Both smiled. "You are a cunning old fox," said Brigham tightly.

"And you are the son of your father," replied Nathan Calver.

Five weeks after the commencement of the sough the tunnel was scarcely two thirds completed. The rock which had been alternately hard, then soft, now seemed to be more compacted and difficult to work. Brett could scarcely make any impression on it with his pick; and even old Seth and Black Jake complained that they could not sense the grain. Every inch of progress represented hours of labour, and though the days had turned chill on the moors, the men working the face of the tunnel wore nothing but cotton drawers, and still the sweat gleamed and glistened on their backs, formed trickling rivulets and soaked their thin pants through.

As day succeeded day with little to show for all their hard work the two men looked increasingly depressed, and in sympathy with them so were the rest of the household at Whistling Clough. Tempers became easily frayed as the possibility of failure grew more certain: Black Jake and Brett had a furious row over which they almost came to blows when Jake accused Brett of not shoring the tunnel walls properly; Brett in his turn had a quarrel with Abby which ended in his cousin's tearful retreat to her room, and even Mrs Hallam was so fretful that she boxed the ears of young Jack when she caught him stealing jam tarts from the larder.

It is doubtful whether any of them could have stood the nervous strain for much longer without the whole project being abandoned in despair and anger, but as fortune would have it their luck turned at the beginning of the sixth week of digging. It was Seth who noticed it first. He gave two or three blows with his pick at the iron hard rock then paused as if listening for something. His wizened, walnut-like countenance was drawn and his pale blue eyes held the light of fifty years' experience underground: he knew the earth and its ways as any ordinary man knows the back of his hand.

"Yon's hollow," he said simply.

Black Jake and Brett, who had been fixing new shoring timbers looked at him incredulously. The flickering light of the working candles danced demon shadows on the tunnel face. Hollow? How could it be? They were still many yards from the mine workings; yards of solid, ingrained limestone. Brett had a moment's suspicion that the hard work and frustration of the past five weeks had turned the old man's head, but Jake took the matter seriously. Like Seth, Black Jake knew the foibles of the underground.

"Art sure?" he demanded brusquely.

"Aye. Her's a foot or two back—but her's hollow reet enough."

Black Jake quivered with excitement as the full meaning of the news bore in on him. "By God!" he cried. "Then we might do it yet, lads! yon's a cavern o'some sort, and if it runs in t'reet direction then we're made!"

He lifted a pick and took a mighty swipe at the face. Infected by his enthusiasm Seth, too, began to hack away at the rock, whilst Brett could only stand and wonder at it all—the face was not big enough to allow three to work on it at the same time.

Bit by bit they hacked away the stubborn rock until suddenly Black Jake's pick met no resistance. His blow smashed through the thin curtain of limestone to reveal a dark hole beyond. As he broke through a sudden blast of cold air swept from the hole, like a genii escaping from a bottle: there was a soft 'ahh' and the candle flames flickered violently, then stillness came once again.

In less than five minutes they had widened the hole sufficiently to crawl through, candles in hand.

It was not a big cavern, but a narrow slot of the sort that Seth called a 'pot hole'. It was damp and rimed with the weird excrescences of limestone so common in the locality, all fluted like organ pipes and stained to various hues by the minerals in the ever-dripping water. As the three astonished explorers pushed on they found the pothole twisted and narrowed, then widened and lowered so that they could hardly stand upright. At one place the way was barred by a filigree curtain of limestone, like a miniature chancel screen. Beautiful though it was, Black Jake smashed it down with one blow of his pick and strode on.

They could scarcely believe their fantastic good

fortune. For weeks they had struggled against the obdurate limestone, and now suddenly, Nature had completed the job for them.

The end of the cavern came at last. It turned at right angles, became a mere slot and funnelled away darkly into the furthest recesses of the earth, doubtless to join up with some other cave system miles away. But they had done well, though only Black Jake knew how well.

He placed his hand against the blank end wall of the tunnel and stroked it almost affectionately.

"By my reckonin'—and ah've been counting mi steps, mark thee—Whistlin' Clough is not moor nor two or three yards further beyond this wall!"

Brett gave a whoop of delight and even Seth permitted himself a smile.

"Then let's dig!" Brett cried, enthusiastically.

But Black Jake held up his hand in warning. "Howd on a bit!" he said sternly. "Th'art forgettin' summat, young Brett. Behind yon wall theer's thousands o'gallons o'flood watter aw ready to coom pourin' out. If we break through now we'd be washed to eternity, mak no mistake!"

Brett looked crestfallen. "I'd forgotten that," he admitted. "But we have to break through somehow. How's it to be done?"

"Wi powder. I mun set up a small keg and a fuse to blast a way through. Once t'wall is weakened t'pressure o'watter on t'other side will do t'rest."

They went back to the house to break the good news to Will and the rest of the family. It was like a black cloud lifting: everyone smiled again, and Will opened a special cask of ale to celebrate the event.

"Ah never thowt as we'd do it," Will confessed, smiling.

"Me nayther," agreed old Seth, "But fortune favours on us."

Black Jake, his massive dirty paw grasping a pewter pot smiled benignly on one and all, like a disreputable Father Christmas. "Tha wanted faith," he said. "Faith i' Black Jake and what he could do when he set a mind to it. Young Brett had faith, and he's been proven reet. Now its aw oe'r bar t'shoutin'. Tomorrer ah'm for Stoney Middleton to buy t'gun-powder and then—boom! Yon mine'll be free. Mark Black Jake's words, gentlemen, in a year's time we'll aw be rich men, and to Hell wi' Nathan Calver and t'Northern Mining Company!"

Brett laughed. "I'll drink to that," he cried.

At eight o'clock next morning Black Jake strode down the track to Middleton Dale, golden guineas jingling in his pocket with which to buy the gun-powder. They were Will Booth's guineas, of course, because Will was paying the bill for the digging of the sough, and though Jake was a partner in the enterprise he had no money of his own. Like old Seth, his contribution was skill and labour. So Will Booth paid, and paid more than he should, because Black Jake lied to him about the cost of powder and the quantity needed. To Jake there was nothing immoral about this: all his life he had lied and cheated, swindled and double-crossed at every opportunity, and it was too much to expect him to alter now, even though he was to share in the profits of the new venture. An extra guinea or two was always welcome, especially when his business could be combined with a visit to the tavern.

The dark, low beamed tap room was almost empty. He bought his draught of ale and a pipe of tobacco and sat in a corner nook.

"Well stop me, if it ain't Black Jake."

There was no mistaking that smooth mocking voice. Jake looked up. Brigham Calver, dandified as ever, was standing by the table looking down at him. Here was the man who had once condemned him to a lingering underground death, a partner who had double-crossed him. But Jake felt no anger, hardly resentment. The past was done with and he lived for the opportunities of the present. Except from placing one of his huge hands over the top of his tankard, he showed no emotion.

Calver laughed, pleasantly. "You can take away your hand from your ale," he said. "I'm not here to drug ye. I would like a word that's all. May I sit down?"

"Help thisel," replied Jake, watchful just the same.

Brigham Calver placed his riding whip on the table, drew off his exquisite gloves and sat facing his old ally.

"And how goes the sough?" he enquired lightly, as though enquiring after the health of some vague relative.

"Well enough," replied Jake.

"That's not what I hear. The villagers call it

Booth's Folly; they say that it will never be completed."

"Happen."

Brigham considered this enigmatic reply. From the moment he had sighted Black Jake walking down the village street his mind had been sharply working on the meaning of it. Two things were possible—either the sough had been abandoned, or there had been some unexpected development—why else would Jake be away from the mine? That it had not been abandoned was now obvious. There must have been some sudden breakthrough—perhaps they were on the point of winning through. He had followed Jake, seen him purchase the keg of gunpowder and leave it at the store.

"There's time for a man to change his mind," Calver said smoothly.

Black Jake looked at him, his great craggy face expressionless. "Th'art wrong theer," he said cautiously. Calver's heart slipped a beat. "You mean—the sough is finished? 'Tis not possible!"

" 'Tis possible reet enough, Mester Brigham, and 'tis true an aw. We broke through to a cave system and aw we hev to do is blast down t'final wall. So now tha knows: we've won—and theer's nowt tha con do about it."

Never had Calver's cunning mind worked so quickly as it did at that moment. It looked as though Brett Assheton had won. There was only one possible chance to turn the tables, one weak spot—the huge villain who sat opposite.

"Powder can be put to other purposes," Calver

said hurriedly. "It can blow things up as well as blast them down!"

Jake looked at him contemptuously. "Th'art a black hearted devil, Mester Brigham, and as cunning as a fox. Why should I blow up yon sough? T'would be cuttin' me own throat. Ah'm a shareholder in yon mine."

Brigham licked his lips nervously. "What share? A fifth, a quarter? Look—we'll give ye a third; there'll be only thee, me and my father in on it. What says you?"

"Ah've had thy promises afore, Mester Brigham."

"All right, I admit I did ye an injustice—but this matter is serious. That sough must be stopped!"

"Aye, well accidents con happen—'specially wi' gunpowder."

"Exactly. You catch my drift precisely."

"But accidents are dangerous, Mester Brigham. It taks moor than a few promises to mak an accident happen."

Brigham Calver fumbled in his pocket and drew out a fine leather purse which he threw on the table. "There's twenty guineas there," he said, "and one third share to come, when we drain the mine."

Black Jake put the purse carefully into his capacious pocket. The deal was agreed.

CHAPTER NINE

Friends and Enemies

BRIGHAM CALVER RODE hard for Eyam to tell his father what had taken place. He clattered into the cobbled yard, sprang from the saddle, and rushed to the drawing room without bothering to remove his riding boots.

As Brigham blurted out the news, his father's face grew serious and at the end of the tale he seemed displeased.

"I don't like this business with Black Jake," he said sharply. "The man's a rogue. You had no right of offer him a share in the mine."

Brigham snorted angrily. "What else could I do to get him on our side?" he demanded, and added smoothly, "You surely don't imagine I intend to honour the agreement?"

"Knowing you, I imagine not," his father answered. "But there is a more technical problem. If Black Jake blows the tunnel there is always the possibility he might release the flood waters by accident. The blast from powder is a peculiar thing —it sometimes strikes where it was least intended, which is why miners do not like to use it. If he does release the flooding, then we have lost for sure." He paused, a worried look on his face. "But you are right in one respect—the fact that the sough is near completion means we must take urgent action."

"Then what do you suggest?"

"Did anyone see Jake carrying the powder away?"

"Half the village, I imagine. He strode down the street with the keg on his shoulder."

"Good! Then we must rouse the populace to its danger!"

"Danger? What danger? I do not follow you, Sir."

"You'll see! Get the ostler to saddle my horse. We must ride for Stoney Middleton at once!"

Edward Morton, Barmaster of the Liberty, was surprised at the disturbed appearance of his distinguished visitor.

"Why Dr Denman!" he exclaimed. "What ails thee—tha looks aw of a bother."

Joseph Denman was fat and flabby and not given to exercise. That he should ever try to run was something remarkable, for it made him red-faced and out of breath, not at all becoming to a man of his status. Dr Denman was not only the local doctor, but a Justice of the Peace and related by marriage to the Fynneys, an influential local family. His dignity was something he prized, so that to see him throw it away by trying to run was indeed surprising.

"Ah! Oh! Dear me—my breath, y'know," gasped Dr Denman as Morton helped him into a chair. "Running—bad for a man in my condition." He panted heavily for a few seconds, then, as if recalling the purpose of his hurried visit, blurted out,

"We must stop it, sir! Stop it at once!" And he ended with a paroxysm of coughing which left him purple in the face.

"Stop what?"

"Eh? Ah, yes! The meeting. Ugly mob. Nasty crowd. All young Calver's fault."

Morton's long face grew hard. "Tha means theer's a mob i' Stoney. For what purpose?"

"Mining trouble. Came to you immediately. Not sure how I stand, and all that. I mean, J.P. and so forth, must keep the peace—but demned tricky when miners are involved, eh?"

"What miners, and what's t'trouble?" demanded the Barmaster, becoming exasperated at his visitor's disjointed account.

"Whole village as far as I could see. Demned rascals the lot of 'em. They're out for mischief and they've got to be stopped!"

Morton could sense the urgency of the situation even though he had no notion of what the doctor was trying to tell him. Without waiting for further explanation he grabbed his hat and made for the door.

"Here! Wait for me," cried Dr Denman—but the Barmaster had gone. "Demned uncivil fellow!" protested the fat doctor, flopping back exhausted into his chair.

The Barmaster strode purposefully down the street. He had no need to ask direction for he could hear the sound of an angry multitude gathered by the bridge. As he rounded a corner he could tell at a glance that Denman had been right in one respect. Almost the whole village was present, men and

women, and they were roused as he had never seen
them roused before.

He thrust his way through the crowd. Nathan and
Brigham Calver were standing on a stone wall and
had obviously just finished speaking. At the sight of
the Barmaster, the noise fell away like a receding
tide to hushed, angry murmur.

"What is aw this, Mesters?" demanded Morton,
in a strong stern voice, addressing the Calvers.

"Ah! Barmaster—glad you have come. We would
have sent for you had there been time. There is the
likelihood of grave trouble at Whistling Clough."
Nathan Calver was polite to the point of excess. It
grated on the Barmaster's plain nature.

"Trouble? We have a Court to deal wi trouble,
Mester Calver, as well tha knows. What's t'meaning
o'this mob?"

"A Barmote Court would be too late, Barmaster,"
Brigham said. "The fact is that Black Jake o'Lang-
sett is intent on blasting through to the flooded
Bottom Level with gunpowder."

The Barmaster nodded. "Ah guessed as much
mesel'," he said. "Ah seed him wi a keg o'powder
this morn. But what has that to do wi aw this?"

"He'll flood us out o'house an' home, that's
what!" cried a voice from the crowd. An angry
murmur of assent rose.

"They speak the truth," said Brigham. "My
father and I have examined the mine—we had a
passing interest in it as you may recall—and there
are thousands of gallons of water locked in the
galleries. Once that is released it will sweep down

Whistling Clough like a tidal wave until it reaches Middleton Dale. There it will turn and dash down upon the village. Everything will be lost—the smelting house, the inns, the church, houses—aye, the very bridge we meet at now will be swept away!"

There was a howl of anger from the mob. Morton glanced about him: the Dale was narrow, confined between walls of limestone a hundred feet high, so narrow indeed that there was scarcely room for the road, the little river and the houses, which pressed with their backs against the crags. *It could happen,* he thought. The dale would act like one big funnel for the released waters of the mine.

"Will Booth's a sensible chap," he protested. "If there was ony danger he'd ne'er let it happen."

"That's true enough," shouted someone. "Will's a good chap."

But Brigham Calver stamped out any sympathy there might have been for Will Booth immediately. "Booth is in no danger," he cried. "His house stands well above the clough—and in any case he is no longer in charge. I grant you that Will Booth is a grand fellow—but can we say the same of that rascal of a nephew, Brett Assheton? Aye, and his villainous partner, Black Jake!"

Another howl came from the enraged mob.

"They want lead," shouted Brigham, "and they don't care how they get it! What's it to them if the village is swamped!"

"Hang 'em!" cried a voice. "Let 'em swing!"

"Even at this moment they may be setting the fuse," Brigham yelled.

It was enough. With a wild surge the crowd broke and began to run towards Whistling Clough. Brigham Calver was for running with them but his father laid a restraining hand on his arm. "Let the fools run," he said softly. "We must not appear to lead them."

Black Jake's arrival at the mine with the gun-powder was greeted by loud hurrahs. Everyone from the house had come to watch the final blow that would free Whistling Clough, even Granny Booth and Mrs Hallam. A large hamper of provisions had been brought up by Jack and Wilf, and the intention was to make a picnic out of the event.

Much to Brett's surprise, Black Jake insisted on placing the charge and laying the train of gun-powder which would act as a fuse, by himself.

"This is dangerous work, lad," he said gruffly. "Ah'm t'chap as knows just how it mun be placed, so tha mun let me do it. Theer's no caw to risk other lives. Everyone else mun stay out o' t'sough."

"Well if you say so," Brett agreed. He had grown fond of the huge villain, respected his craftsmanship and trusted his judgement. That Black Jake should alone be responsible for the blasting of the final wall seemed to Brett perfectly reasonable.

So Jake carried the keg into the sough whilst the others waited outside, anxious for the job to be finished and their dreams realised.

Suddenly they heard the drumbeat of fast-flying hooves and looked up in surprise.

" 'Tis the Barmaster!" exclaimed Abby, her

sharp eyes first to see the swift moving figure on the brown landscape. "And he's riding Dr Denman's best mare!"

Now they could all see the horseman. He was swift and careless on the rough moor, giving the mare her head when a more cautious man would have held a tight rein.

"He'll break his neck ridin' like yon!" exclaimed Will, concerned. "The chap's demented."

With a flurry that sent the peat flying, the Barmaster skidded his horse swiftly down the flanks of the clough, then dashed crazily through the boulder-strewn brook until he fetched up with a sudden halt at the mining party.

"The village is roused!" he cried, springing from the saddle. "Calver has towd 'em a tale as how th'art gooin' to blast t'mine and flood Stoney Middleton. Ah've ridden like the Devil hissel o'er t'top-side to beat 'em and warn thee."

"Many thanks Edward," said Will Booth. "I tak that reet kindly."

"It's nobbut my job as Barmester to keep t'peace among miners. Ah'll try and talk to 'em agen, Will, but ah'm afeerd they mean trouble. They're out for t'wreck yon sough."

Abby gave a sudden little scream and pointed down the clough. A rabble of villagers, some armed with staves, were noisily picking their way up the steep path. The narrowness of the clough had forced them to bunch together, but this if anything, had given them greater determination and even from a distance it was plain to see they were in an ugly mood. At the back of the mob were two riders on horseback, carefully steering their mounts up the steep path.

"Here come the Calvers, waiting like vultures to carry off the meat when the killing's done," said Brett, bitterly. "Well, they'll not destroy the sough without a fight, that I promise!"

Abby ran up to him and flung her arms about his neck sobbing. "Don't fight, Brett, don't fight!" she implored. "There are too many of them and they are so angry you'll be killed for sure."

He smiled at her, put his arm round her waist and gave her a comforting hug.

"You told me once that it was only lead that mattered at Whistling Clough."

"Lives are more important than lead—your life especially," she replied.

The Barmaster agreed with Abby. "Feightin's to no avail lad," he said. "Even Brett Assheton cawn't tak on a whole village."

At that moment Black Jake emerged from the tunnel, laying the last few feet of the powder trail. At the sound of the villagers he turned and stared in amazement.

"What i' Hades—!" he exploded. Then he saw the Calvers and his face twisted into a sardonic grin.

Brigham Calver had dismounted and come to the front of the crowd, which had gathered at the foot of the bing heaps from the mine. His voice echoed from the sides of the clough, like a prophet of doom.

"We've come to stop the blasting of the sough,"

he shouted. "We are not going to stand by and see the village drowned."

Black Jake strode to the edge of the bing heaps and glanced down at Calver and the mob. They recoiled instinctively, out of fear of this gigantic man. Brett, watching, could understand their feelings. Black Jake was a fearsome sight at the best of times, but now, stripped to the waist, with his great hairy barrel chest and his massive arms matted with black powder, he looked the very impersonation of the Devil himself.

"Theer's to be no floodin'," he boomed. "Ne'er mind what Brigham Calver tells thee. Black Jake o'Langsett built this sough, and that is guarantee for ony mon! Now goo whoam to thi childer!"

There were murmurs of irresolution at this. Though Black Jake was hated, his ability as a sougher was known and respected. Calver, however, did not let the matter rest there.

"What!" he cried. "Are we to take the word of a drunken sheep-stealer? Are we to believe a rogue like Black Jake when our homes are at stake? What does he care if the water floods the village as long as he gets his share of the mine!"

Black Jake's face contorted in fury. "By God! Ah'll do for thee Calver, if ah swings for it!" he cried, and with a great leap sprang down the steep bing heap towards his enemy.

But Calver was too quick for him. The dandy thrust a hand into the pocket of his exquisite riding jacket and drew out a small, silver handled pistol. Jake, blind with rage, ignored all danger and came on like a mad bull. There was a sharp *crack*! a little wisp of blue smoke drifted lazily from the muzzle of the pistol and the great hulk of Black Jake crashed forwards like a felled oak. He rolled once, twice, down the loose rubble, then lay still.

The crowd, appalled, shrank back in horror. Brett, Morton and old Seth jumped down the slippery spoil heap as one man, and whilst the Barmaster and the old miner tenderly lifted the body of Black Jake to carry it to a more comfortable place, Brett went for Calver like a tiger.

Calver had no time to reload, so he flung the pistol at his adversary, missed, and came in to grapple. Brett hit him a stunning blow to the jaw, but Calver managed to half ride it and counter attacked with a punch to the stomach. Brett's knees sagged momentarily and he felt like retching, but self preservation learned in dozens of similar fights made him hit back furiously. He smashed his right fist savagely into Calver's face and followed it with a left to the head.

It was not a pretty fight to watch. There was no artistry, no skill such as a trained prize-fighter might use—just anger and savagery. Nothing was barred; fists, knees, boots, went in regardless, and within minutes both contestants were covered with a frightening veneer of dirt and blood. Still they fought on, watched by the mob. Nobody interfered because it was a fair fight, animal against animal, and to interfere would be like breaking some primeval custom.

The two contestants struggled in the muddy clough, and up the steep bing slopes, first one giving ground, then the other as the advantage swayed to and fro. Eventually they were fighting at the very entrance to the sough, as though each had fought his way to claim the cause of the dispute.

Suddenly Calver stumbled and for a moment his guard went down. Remorselessly Brett whipped his right hand across his opponent's jaw, and Calver fell like a pole-axed ox.

Brett leant against the sough entrance wall, breathing heavily. When he spoke he was out of breath and his voice was half choking, half sobbing, but a voice of command.

"Enough of this nonsense!" he gasped. "The flint! Light the fuse!"

Abby came forward with a tinder box which she gave to Brett. He stooped swiftly and struck a spark to the trail of black powder. It hissed and spluttered in a shower of sparks, then catching light, ran sizzling into the recesses of the tunnel.

"He's lit t'fuse!" cried a panic-stricken voice. "Quick! Out o't'clough afore t'watter ketches us!"

There was a mad scramble as the villagers stumbled up the steep grass bank of the clough to avoid the rushing waters which they knew must come at any moment.

Brigham Calver recovered consciousness and staggered to his feet just in time to see the villagers rushing up the slopes. From the mouth of the sough he glanced up to where Brett was now standing, arms akimbo.

"Get out of the sough Calver!" Brett cried. "I've lit the fuse and she'll blow any minute."

Calver gave a wild demented laugh. "Fools!" he yelled at the top of his voice. "Fools the lot o'ye! D'ye think a Calver can be beaten that easily?" And he gave another wild laugh, as though enjoying some enormous private joke.

"Come away from the sough!" cried Brett anxiously. "I've lit the fuse man! Don't you understand?"

"I understand well enough, Brett Assheton," Calver cried. "But it signifies nothing. You think you will blow open the sough, but you won't. *You'll close it!*"

A sudden pang of apprehension gripped Brett's throat. "What do you mean?" he cried.

"I mean that Black Jake had changed sides again and was working with me. He planted the powder not where it would release the water, but where it would fetch down the roof and seal your precious tunnel for ever!"

Suddenly Brett felt tired and sick. So that was it! That was why Jake insisted that nobody should watch him set the charge. Anger, humiliation, both fought for control of his emotions. What a fool he had been to trust a knave like Black Jake! What right had he to believe that a man like that could feel anything but greed? There had seemed some indefinable common bond between them, something stronger than greed or material gain, something of a kindred spirit. He was *sure* of it—yet it was not so. Like Judas, Black Jake had sold out for thirty pieces of silver.

His melancholy thoughts were interrupted by a

sudden dull *boom*! in the depths of the sough. There followed a low rumbling as though the earth was complaining of the disturbance.

Calver gave another wild laugh. "There goes your sough, Master Assheton, and with it your hopes! Whistling Clough will be a Calver mine after all!"

But Brett wasn't listening. He was watching with horrified fascination a narrow ribbon of black water snaking out of the mouth of the tunnel.

"Look out!" he cried.

Calver turned, saw the water, and with a wild despairing leap, sprang for the sides of the spoil heap. But he was a fraction too late. The earth rumbled and shook and then with terrible suddenness, a wall of water, carrying boulders and timbers as if they were matchsticks, burst from the mouth of the tunnel and went roaring down into Whistling Clough. Calver had no chance. The water caught him, plucked him into its embrace, tossed him up amidst the grinding boulders like a plaything and hurled him into the clough. He disappeared completely, swiftly, silently, carried by the tumultuous flood to Middleton Dale.

Brett was shocked. Dimly he was aware of shouts and tumult, of women screaming and men cursing, but it was like another world. He watched the tumbling water subside to a steady flow, as the first release spent itself, but he felt no elation. He heard cheering, and was aware not only that he had won, but that the village was safe. Black Jake had calculated correctly.

Slowly he wandered over to where the body of

Jake lay stretched on a patch of late heather. Even in death the face looked as villainous as ever, dirty, unkempt.

He felt remorse that he had ever doubted this huge, shambling giant. There *had* been more than greed after all—or was it that Jake had intended to double-cross Calver all along. Certainly he had placed the powder where he said he would. He had blown the wall.

Old Seth wandered up.

"I thought he'd done for us Seth," said Brett, simply.

The old miner shook his head. "Nay lad, 'twere never on," he said slowly. "He were a villain and a rogue reet enough, but he were a grand sougher, a master on his craft. Dust tha think he would hev destroyed his own handiwork? Why, Calver could've gi'en him t'moon and he'd ne'er do that!"

Brett turned away. He felt tears welling up in his eyes, pricking and hurting. He had not cried since he was a small child and he fought against it.

He told himself he had won, the mine was his and he would be rich. But he still felt like crying, for his heart told him he had lost, lost something he had come to love dearly.

Abby came up and slipped her arm around him. She understood. A sudden spasm of rage swept over him.

"I hate lead!" he cried violently. "Hate it! Hate it!"

"That's the way of it, Brett dearest," said Abby softly.